Born to Survive

Will to Live

By Anthony G. Pasqualetti

authorHOUSE™

1663 LIBERTY DRIVE, SUITE 200
BLOOMINGTON, INDIANA 47403
(800) 839-8640
WWW.AUTHORHOUSE.COM

First published by AuthorHouse 05/27/05

ISBN: 1-4208-4602-7 (sc)

Library of Congress Control Number: 2005903608

Printed in the United States of America
Bloomington, Indiana

This book is printed on acid-free paper.

Acknowledgement

I would like to thank the many people

in my life who made my journey rich and fulfilling.

To each of you, Thank you.

Many of the names in my book have been changed

to protect the rights of loved ones

and long-time friends and their families.

Dedication

I dedicate this book to my wife Ida, son Anthony, and daughter Patricia; and to my brothers, Frank, Lewis and Bobby; and sisters, Francis and Julie; to cousin Rosalyn, who inspired me to write my life story, stating: "What a rich life you had. Most guys would have one or two incidents. You came up with story after story. Most guys would love to have lived your life."

I would also like to recognize my grandchildren and great grandchildren who will have my story as a legacy to our family. Also to my niece Rosemary who assisted with the early stages of my book, and to Barbara LaGrange for her proofreading and type setting skills.

I also dedicate my story to my mother who passed away at the age of 99 in the year 2002. She was a wonderful mother who had a very tough life and bore 13 children. I am sorry she will never read this book.

Contents

List of Photographs

1. Army photo: front cover of book, holding New York State Conspicuous Service Cross by Gov. Nelson Rockefeller; and Army Bronze Star

2. Mother and Father: Gaetono and Mary Pasqualetti

3. My photo at four years old

4. Our marriage: Ida and Anthony Pasqualetti

5. Bicycle accident in Buffalo, New York

6. Cook at Veterans Hospital: Buffalo, New York

7. Our 40th Anniversary

8. Security Officer: U.S. Post Office

9. Two spinal infusions: 1971 and 1973

10. Past member Lions Club; Second Vice President

11. 50th Anniversary photo

12. Picture of us and son, Anthony, and daughter, Patricia, who paid for our 50th Anniversary cruise

13. Mother: Mary Pasqualetti Lepkowski

14. Cut hand on band saw

15. Our 56th Anniversary: Gulf Port, Mississippi, same time as my reunion

16. 58th year reunion with my combat outfit: 85th Div. 339 Regiment at Gulf Port, Mississippi

17. Photo of Liberty Ship similar to one I sailed on overseas; our daughter paid for our trip to San Francisco as our 58th Anniversary gift. Wife and daughter standing on the spot I laid on when attacked by German aircraft on April, 11, 1944.

18. Eye implants: two on left and one on right

19. 58th year reunion with combat outfit: Washington DC

20. Back Cover photo: 50th Anniversary

21. Hand-crafted a fort as a pool table lamp

22. Made Ghost Trees for Halloween

23. Designed and built a home bar

24. Designed a family heirloom: a Christmas Crèche

Chapter One
The Early Years

My first day of life began on August 11, 1924 on Swan Street in Buffalo, New York. My father was a native of Italy but my mother was an Italian-American and was born in Raritan, New Jersey.

Being the second born child, as well as a sickly baby, did not stop Mother from having eleven more children. My father's trade was in fireworks. He couldn't read or write English; he used an ink stamp with his name on it to sign papers. Dad knew his trade better than anyone I knew. His fireworks were usually of images. I remember vividly there were two roosters fighting each other, and one of Niagara Falls that showed the water running; he always ended his shows with the American flag that he was so proud of. Dad also worked for the Nickel Plate railroad. My mother once told me that Dad was well known and well liked, and that the Mayor of New York City carried him on his shoulder throughout the streets of New York City.

Being the sick child that I was it took me until I was two years old to take my first steps. My mother used to tell me that I would cry day and night, and occasionally Dad would want to throw me out of the window. I remember her telling me there

1

was one doctor who wanted to perform surgery on my head to see if the problem stemmed from there. I was in such poor shape that I was given last rights twice. One of those times, the doctor told my mother to get a priest because I would be dead by morning. If it wasn't for my godmother, I may have not survived to tell my story. She told my mother to bathe me in a copper tub with hot water laced with dried mustard powder, in order to remove the "sickness" from me. She and my mother wrapped me in towels and blankets and stayed up all night praying. My godmother, with her old Italian ways believed in the "evil eye" but my mother was afraid. By morning, the doctor arrived with the death certificate ready to sign, but instead he was surprised to find that I survived the night. My mother was afraid to tell the doctor what they did, so my godmother explained what transpired. The doctor told both of them that the procedure had saved my life but warned them that I would need a lot of care for a long time. This was my first escape from death. Not knowing at the time, I learned that there would be more close calls to follow in my lifetime.

One sunny morning, I ran out across the streetcar's tracks. I nearly got hit but luckily a young woman grabbed me. The girl caught her dress on the car, which turned out to be a blessing in disguise. If she hadn't ripped her dress she would have been pulled under the car and we both might have been killed.

I will never forget the spanking I received and for a long time I did not pull a stunt like that.

Another time, I was heading to the store with my dad for an ice cream cone. It was the first time in my life that I saw a black person. The person stopped to say 'hello' to us, but I got scared, ran, and dropped my dessert. My dad called me back to tell me that the individual was his friend. The kind gentleman bought me another ice cream after the incident.

I remember when I was about six or seven, I had another brush with death. There was a big, cylinder, tile well that they would use when they put in new wells. I decided to put paper in the cylinder along with a box and I climbed into it. I then lit the paper on fire and the flames got bigger and bigger and I got scared. My friend on the outside of the cylinder yelled for me to get out and he helped pull me out. I fell on broken glass and a small piece of glass imbedded in my lip. My dad tried to stop the bleeding but he was pushing the glass deeper into my lip. My friend noticed what was happening and ran to find my mother. It was my mother who got the glass out and gave me a spanking in the process. To this day, I still have the scar and I never played with matches again. Kids are always getting themselves in trouble and I was no exception. I could have burned to death, but my friend saved me.

I was home alone one morning and I had nothing to do so I put salt in the oven, I could not understand why it was smoking. A neighbor saw the smoke and came in and turned off the oven. He then got my mother from the corner store. My mother looked at me like she could have killed me. I ran from her as I did many times, outside and around the house a couple of times and into the grape field. My mother was so angry she threw a lump of mud at me and it knocked me down. She picked me up and spanked me all the way home. She then tied my hands together and told me if I continued to get into trouble she would keep them tied until it was time to go to bed. My mother untied my hands and put me in the cellar to stay with the rats. Of course, there were no rats but I did not know that at the time. My mother came and checked on me and gave me milk and cookies until it was time for supper, later she sent me to bed. This was a lesson I learned the hard way.

When I was about three years old, my first little sister, Frances died. She was the first dead person I saw. She died because the doctor gave her the wrong medicine. My father threw the doctor down a flight of stairs. At the wake, Frances was laying with colored candies. I was at the casket and told her that she had a lot of candy, so I started to help myself to some of the candy but my mother stopped me and told me the candy was for the angels. About three days after the funeral, my mother told us about a strange thing that happened. Summer after summer, a little yellow canary came to the window where

4

Frances slept and it never missed a day. Mother said it was Frances's angel. When Frances was about a year old she had a toy that was a little yellow canary.

One year, while still living on Swan Street, my father put on a huge display of fireworks for St. Lucy's Church. My brother and I were sitting on the merry-go-round --- the kind you had to push around yourself --- when the fire works started. The crowd glanced towards the sky. Thirty feet above them the Virgin Mary appeared. It was like the earth stood still. Men and women got on their knees and made the sign of the cross. When the Virgin Mary reached the ground, she was in full color with white, blue, and pink for her face for all to see. Just as she appeared, she went back up and faded away.

My mother told me that my father once set up two dummies in my godmother's house. He placed one in each bathroom. My godmother's son did not know this. When he went to the bathroom and opened the door he heard a noise and he saw a strange man in the bathroom. He ran to his mother and said there is a strange man in the bathroom and she told him to use the other bathroom and there, again, was the second dummy.

Dad was a genius when it came to fireworks. I believe I inherited some of his talent in working with wood. My dad was an exceptional human being. He was well known in the Italian community and well known to leaders from New York all the way to Pennsylvania for his fireworks displays. I remember my mother telling us the story that happened in Galenton, Pennsylvania before 1930. A Catholic cemetery was having problems with the Ku Klux Klan. Statues were vandalized through out the entire area. The mayor of the town contacted my father for help. My father, with the help of my godfather and two friends, set up the cemetery with fireworks. As the Klan began destroying plots, my father and his men lit the fireworks. This continued all over the cemetery. The fireworks were not set up to go in the air; they were set at the height of eight feet. The Klan scattered for their lives along with braking legs and arms while fleeing. Dad's heroism put an end to the Klan in Galenton.

My father's health began to fail. His Italian buddies thought that he should return home to his native land. My father, leaving his family behind, took four trunks of clothing with him. After spending a few months in Italy his health deteriorated. He decided to return to the states to his family. It was mid winter and a very bad blizzard had stalled the taxi service; no taxis were running. My dad had to walk a mile to get home and with him being in very bad health, the walking did not do him any good. When he reached the door he kicked it three times and my mother knew it was my dad. In the morning, my mother asked my father where his trunks of clothes and blankets were. He explained he came home with only the clothes on his back because his people kept everything else. My father could not go back to work at the Nickel Plate railroad; his working days were over.

After my father passed away, my mother, my siblings, and I moved to a town called Cooks Corner. Our home sat high on a hill near a house that was reported as haunted. No one lived in the abandoned house but every night a light would turn on. It was too much for my mother once dad was gone so she took us to Galenton, Pennsylvania, to visit some relatives. I recall the uncle could eat one hot pepper after another --- no water or bread. He could eat one or two lemons without making a funny face. When we returned home we discovered our home was broken into. I remember the police officer lifting the attic ceiling board to see if anybody was hiding up there before he left.

The area was farmland and I remember that an older Italian man owned two goats. My siblings and I would laugh when he tried to milk the goats. The poor farmer had trouble milking because they would not stand still for him, so he put two posts in the ground and tied their hind legs to the posts, which allowed him to milk the goats.

I recall my mother was having problems keeping my siblings and me in line. She decided to take us to Father Baker's orphanage. As she was climbing the stairs to the great big door, she said this was where she was going to leave us all if we were not going to behave. It was up to each of us to decide if we would stay there or go back home and behave. The fear of being put in an orphanage worked.

It was difficult for my mother to raise her children by herself with no income and that forced us to move once again. I remember my next residence was in a small town called Lawtons, New York. It was a mile from the Indian reservation border. Our home was behind a grocery store and a post office. To the right was an empty lot and to the right of that was a railroad depot and a saloon on the other side of the tracks. My siblings and I became friends with the saloonkeeper's children. In those days, whiskey was hard to come by. The ABC Board shut our friend's business down once. The owner's seven-year-old daughter gave away her father's secret; she said it was not under the porch.

I will never forget the beating that child received with a water hose. In today's society, the man would be arrested for child abuse and thrown in jail.

After the saloon reopened, my mother took a job working as a cook. Soon after she met my stepfather, Ted Lepkowski. Ted was a musician in a band and played the saxophone.

Living close to the reservation, my brother and I had an experience we have never forgotten. While living in the house, we could see what was going on downstairs by looking through a knothole on the floor. One evening, we saw the landlord having a fight with an Indian. The Indian stabbed the man.

The man was old but he was strong and he beat the hell out of the Indian with a black jack. After the beating, he carried him outside and dumped him a couple of blocks away from the house for the sheriff to find. We heard the Indian was taken to his own native hospital later that day.

Another afternoon my mother sent me out to look for my brother. Instead of finding my brother, I found a woman, who they called Snuffy, drunker than a skunk. I saw many others drunk and fighting as I crossed the empty lot and the tracks on my way to the saloon to find my brother. I could not find him so I started back and again saw Snuffy hiding behind one of the train sheds. I also saw a drunken Indian running down the tracks bleeding from a fight. When I crossed the lot again, there was another bleeding Indian. I did not see him at first because a big pile of posts was blocking him, but he saw me and he started to come after me with a big knife. We were see-sawing on each side of the pile of posts. Just at this time, my brother and his friend were walking down the sidewalk and my brother saw what was going on. He sent his friend to tell our mother.

While he was close to the house, my brother yelled, "You, drunken Indian." When the Indian turned to look at my brother, I figured I would make a run for it. I thought I could run faster than the Indian could run because he was very drunk and I ran like fire. Just as I closed the door, the knife came through it.

My brother was all ready up the stairs and he did not see the knife come through the door. The next thing I heard was the most terrible scream I have ever heard in my life. My mother threw a pot of hot boiling water on the Indian from the upstairs window. That was the last time I saw the Indian and I bet that sobered him up. My mother always kept pots of hot boiling water.

Our school was just a one-room structure painted fire engine red. Since we had no vehicle at that time, my brother's and I had to walk at least a mile along the highway to attend school. It made no difference if it was winter or summer. I remember our teacher, Mrs. Rogers, with a great fondness. She had no children of her own but she always enjoyed doing nice things for her students. She baked me a birthday cake and that was her first attempt at making devil's food cake. I will never forget that. During classes she often told her students the stories of Admiral Byrd and his adventure's at the North Pole.

One day after school, three bullies picked on my older brother. He would not fight back and went home crying to our mother. I received a spanking but I will never understand why because I was not with him. Our mother taught us something we have never forgotten: "Do not start any fights, but fight back if they start first." The next day I heeded her words because I was so mad at the spanking I received for something I did not do. I beat the hell out of each kid who beat my brother and I never said anything to my mother but she had a way of finding out these things. She never did lecture me again about fighting and everything was fine in school after that. I was not a bully but I began to stick up for what I believed in.

The town's sheriff's son, Howard, constantly called me "Neno," an Italian slang for Anthony. I continued to tell him I did not like it. Did he listen? No. I knew the only thing I could do was to knock him down and rub his face in the snow. He had a mole that started to bleed and he ran home crying. Howard and I became good friends after that.

We knew a rancher near by who raised prize winning Black Angus and bulls. One afternoon, he caught me in his apple tree and scolded me for being on his property. I remember telling him I wasn't stealing but that the tree was in the empty lot. He was more afraid that I would fall from his tree. After that he gave me an apple and later visited our home and delivered some apples to our mother. I will always remember the kindness that the rancher and his mother showed to my family. He never had any sons of his own, and one day he asked our mother if he could take us to the fair --- he even offered to give us money to spend. I'll always remember his mother and the black ribbon she used to wear around her neck. She was such a kind woman. She would ask me to bring her the paper after school then she would give me an ice cream cone every night.

Many years later after I married my wife, Ida, she and our son returned to the town to see if the farm was still there. Of course, the rancher and his family were deceased by this time but we met his son who was born shortly after we moved. This young man was the local veterinarian. He was kind enough to give us a tour of the area. It was the first time our young son was exposed to many different farm animals.

While I still lived in Lawtons, one of my pals and I dressed up for another Halloween night as cowboys, complete with cap guns, cowboy hats and boots --- you name it, we had it. We were so proud of our costumes, thinking that we were the Real McCoys or at least we thought we did. I remember knocking on our neighbor's house and said, "This is a stick up! Tricks or treats!" The husband was a retired railroad worker and every Sunday they would give me the paper to bring home. He said we scared his wife and there won't be any more Sunday paper.

We made another move, one of many, but this time it was much closer to school. I remember the owner told my mother the red house was over 100 years old. One evening, while we were sitting down for supper, a cat appeared in the upper window of the kitchen and jumped in and landed on my dinner plate, much to everyone's surprise. I had no idea what was happening until my stepfather shouted, "Get away from the table. That cat has rabies." The cat was facing me, snarling. My stepfather, Ted, got his gun and shot at the cat twice. The cat ran outside the same way that it had entered. Ted went outside and put seven bullets in the poor cat before it died. I found out later it was burned up and then buried.

One day when I got home from school, Mother asked me what I did with the bread from the neighbor's porch. My brother had run home and told Mother that I stole a loaf of bread. Mother mentioned the family name where the loaf of bread had been stolen. I said that I didn't come home that way. The road was in a shape of a "horseshoe" and you entered from the highway and it brings you right back to the highway. However, my brother kept putting more fuel on the fire by saying, "Tell Ma and I will give you my bow and arrow." I used a new word that I had learned in school that day --- denied --- not knowing what it meant so I used it. I always laugh when under pressure or blamed for something, so Mother figured I did it.

I got beat from room to room, top of the bed, under the bed. My brother got a kick out of this and went to tell all of his friends about the beating. I got a lot of spankings on account of my brother. Later, the Sheriff found out about the stolen bread and my beating. The Sheriff came to see Mother and said: "Your son did not steal the loaf of bread. He is a good boy. He doesn't steal or fight unless he is picked on. It was my son and another boy."

Mother's reply was: "This is what he will get if he steals."

Mother had a tough role with a bunch of kids and she did whatever it took to keep us honest. Mother was a good mother and kept us out of trouble.

In the thirties, the Depression was on and it was hard times for Americans, and few jobs for the men. Men without work were more like boys without discipline. One Halloween night, the kids were lookouts and got the attention of the farm owners while the jobless men knocked down hay stacks that the farmers had just stacked, or were known to push hay wagons into school yards to block the school doors. They also managed to get a hay wagon on the railroad depot roof. Many outhouses were knocked over, including ours. This time our landlord was going to protect our outhouse so he sat inside with a shotgun filled with rock salt. The men came by and lassoed the outhouse that was then hooked up to a tractor. The outhouse fell over, the shotgun went off and the landlord landed in the stinking "honeydew". For the next couple of weeks those men had some work restacking hay and building outhouses. The following year was a different story. All the farmers had shotguns loaded with rock salt. There were some sore behinds and the end of Halloween mischief.

There were three Catholic families in the town of Lawtons, New York. It was another Halloween night. The Klan figured a woman with a few kids would be an easy target. Mother was informed about the Klan. The Klan didn't like Catholics; Mother was ready for them.

The front of our house had a porch with four posts. I remember that some Klan members started to climb the post to get to the roof. From the porch roof they could come through the window and attack my mother and the children. Mother was one step ahead of them. Mother was on the roof with her pots of boiling water, waiting for them. As soon as they got their arms on the roof, Mother let them have it. They all fell back to the ground. In the morning, Mother went to the grocery store and she saw that the two store owner's had their hands wrapped up and their faces reddened from the douse of hot water. Then she saw the postmaster and the garage owner all wrapped up. Whether they had their hoods on or off, Mother knew who they were. Then she told the other Catholic families before she notified the Buffalo District Attorney and gave all of the names of the Klan. If anything happened to her and her children or any of the families, they would be arrested. That was the end of the Klan in Lawtons, New York.

I wasn't always the best brother in our big family. Once while Mother was baking cupcakes, I asked my sister, Frances, to give me her index finger, placing it on the hot cupcake. Of course, she screamed, and that's all my mother needed to hear.

This time I ran under the bed but Mother had a new weapon --- a board with nine straps on it. She didn't know at first that I was hanging on to the springs of the bed, away from the floor. When she realized it where I had been hiding, she became even angrier and proceeded to give me a good strapping. She also placed my finger on the cupcake to see if I liked it but by then they were cool, so I screamed anyway. My poor sister also got a swat for being stupid enough to listen to me in the first place.

The welfare department sent one of their social workers to our home. She wanted to adopt me but my mother wouldn't allow it. The woman was able to convince my mother to let me stay with her and her family for a few days. Those few days turned into two weeks. I remember Mrs. Murphy had a daughter who was approximately fifteen years old, and she along with her father, wanted me to live with them. Thanks to my mother, it was never to be. Once again, after I married, I took Ida to the headquarters of the welfare department to seek legal advice. My wife and I were trying to help a young girl who was mistreated by her father. We were told how to handle the situation, and they helped make a huge difference in the young woman's life. As I began talking to one of the clerks, Mrs. Murphy overheard the conversation and came out of her office. She stared at me for a long moment and asked if I was Anthony. When I said 'yes', she came over and gave me the biggest hug. I couldn't believe it was the same woman who wanted to adopt me years earlier.

My younger years were full of changes. We soon moved to a little farm town in Brant, New York. In the summer months, Mother would earn money by picking strawberries for half a cent a quart. She was one of the fastest pickers the farm had, and would pick at least four hundred quarts a day. When strawberry season ended, we had blackberries and green beans to pick; in early fall grapes and tomatoes. I often wondered how my mother managed to work in the blazing sun, come home at the end of the day, cook for her husband and children then clean the house and still have time to go over homework with us. Talk about amazing super-woman, my Mother was that, and more!

Ted worked as a handyman not far from where we lived. We did not get along. He knew I never cared for him, and the feeling was mutual. On weekends he would make my brother, Frank, drive him into Lawtons in order for him to play his saxophone at the saloon. He knew full well that my brother did not have a license or even a permit.

In order to keep warm in the winter months, we would take the seats out of Ted's Model-T Ford, chop wood and load the car. The home that Mother and Ted rented was behind an apple orchard and a bee farm. Bees were not active in the winter so my brother and I would take out a slab of honeycomb from the boxes, chew on the comb, return the slabs back into the box then walk home.

Indoor plumbing was a rarity so we needed an outhouse. The folks who worked the fields behind us would also use it. I remember talking to a little girl while her parents worked in the fields. Who would know that years later that same little girl and I would meet again.

Our home, like many others, had no electricity. We used a natural gas mantle on the wall. Our cellar had just a dirt floor, and when it rained we would use a galvanized tub to paddle our way to the pantry shelves to bring canned goods up to the kitchen.

One Fourth of July I had a close call with a firecracker, nearly loosing three of my fingers. The kids who lived nearby in the shanties saw the whole thing and ran home leaving me there.

On another afternoon, as my stepfather was returning home from work, a nearby truck blew out a tire causing the team of horses to panic. Ted was dragged underneath the wagon but only suffered minor scrapes and bruises.

Soon after, we moved to Angola, New York, a town located north of Brant. Mother continued to do menial labor working on the farm as well as in the canning factory. I can't even begin to imagine how hot it must have been for her in those summer months. Any child becomes bored in those lazy days of summer; I was no exception. There was one time when a buddy and I decided to cross a high creek. We figured the only way to get on the other side was to climb the high bank and walk underneath the railroad bridge. We would do this just for fun and usually made it across without mishaps. One day we were not so lucky. We heard the approach of an on-coming train. We quickly grabbed the metal beams underneath the bridge and held on for dear life. The vibration of the train stayed in our minds for quite awhile and it was the last time we pulled a stunt like that. But did it keep us out of mischief? Hell, no!

At the end of York Street stood a huge cement wall. Be hind the wall was a hundred-foot drop to the creek below. Left of the wall was a garage where we would pitch pennies. Sometimes the coins would roll back and go over the edge of the bank, right where a big branch was jutting out. Somehow we dug a cave on the other side of it. We would tie a rope to the branch, pitch our pennies and try to catch them as they went over. But we were always saved by the branch and swung to safety. We managed to fool the other kids, having them believe we fell all the way down, scaring them enough not to come back to our playground. My brother, Lewis, fell one time and I remember he got scratched up pretty bad. We also did other crazy things as children; such as, catching crabs and boiling them in a tin can to watch them turn red but I don't recall if I ate any.

The beach was only three miles from our home and hitch hiking was easy, so we had no problem catching a ride. One particular time, I had another scare of my life. The tavern's daughter was a friend of mine who got even with me after I pulled a prank on her. She told me to dive in the direction of the shore and she would dive in after me because I couldn't swim. Instead, she held me under with her foot until I nearly ran out of air. She then proceeded to tell me: "See what happens when you're being a clown and funny?" Believe me, I never played a prank on her again. It certainly scared the hell out of me, more so than the other incidents in my life. I was just glad she was a friend.

Chapter Two
On My Own

As I got older, my height stayed shorter than most boys my age. I was supposed to go to Fort Erie and train as a jockey. Mother was against it so I quit school at sixteen years old and went to join the Civilian Conservation Corps --- a work program known also as the CCC. I remember my history teacher trying to talk me out of it but she did keep in touch with me while I was away from home. She always told me that I was well advanced for my age, and hated to see me waste it. How smart was I? I was the one who told her who her spouse would be before she even knew!

While in CCC camp, and being away from home for the first time, it was strange for awhile, especially since some of the young men had criminal records. I felt I was accomplishing something: helping families, fighting fires, helping folks who were flooded from their homes, and moving them to the hospitals afterward. Fighting forest fires is very difficult and dangerous, but it didn't stop me! I was small and agile. I would climb to the top of the tree and cut off the burning tops. The camp dentist appreciated my work, picking me as his helper and later picking me to be in charge of the PX. Once I became a senior leader then my pay went from thirty dollars a month to forty-five. I moved out of the barracks and began living in the PX building. It helped make a young man out of me --- something that I will never forget.

I was also a smart businessman in those days. We were about twenty miles from the nearest town and there wasn't much to do at the camp as far as recreation went. We only had one ping-pong table for the two hundred men in camp. I decided to go to the captain with a list of all items that were on sale and applied a five-cent increase on each of them. I figured a five-cent increase wouldn't hurt the men and when we raised enough money we could use it to purchase a pool table and a second ping-pong table. Although I said that the prices would go back to what they were, it never happened because one of the officers didn't like the fact that I separated the money instead of him.

One day, we all had some time off and decided to go swimming. My buddy, who I nicknamed, Knobby, wanted me to dive in but I told him I didn't know how to swim. I still had memories of the incident with my friend back in Angola. He promised me that he would watch me but as I dove in my head hit a rock. I guess the guys thought I was faking it until knobby shouted to the others that I was not moving ... again my life was spared.

Another close call I had was trying to learn how to ice skate. I thought I was doing pretty well until one of my buddies came out of nowhere and pulled me off my feet to slide away from a huge hole in the ice I hadn't seen.

Weighing at 110 pounds, I insisted on trying my hand at boxing. I boxed in about fifteen fights and won all but two.

I remember a cold winter day in December, the 7th of 1941 to be exact. I was heading over to bring the captain the PX cash from the register when they announced over the radio that Pearl Harbor was under attack. The next day all members of the CCC camp began training in dismounted drill formation. In order to leave the camp you had to show proof of employment, so I got a job at a gas station near our house.

When I was released from CCC camp at the tender age of 17, I bought my first car. It was a 1932 Ford from one of my friends, only because the police were after him for speeding in it. One night, while sitting in the local diner, an officer walked up to me and said: "I don't see Jim and I noticed his car is sitting out front in the parking lot."

I told him that I had bought the vehicle. He warned me to be careful since the police in the town had their eye out for it. My friend, also named Frank, would drive with me in the evenings since I only had a learner's permit. One night, I decided to visit my mother who now lived in Buffalo, New York. When she discovered I drove she became upset and insisted that Frank drive us both back, as it was getting dark. We were about seven miles from home taking a bend in the road when suddenly, out of nowhere, a truck came barreling down on us because he had lost a tire. Frank slammed on the brakes and turned the wheel too sharp. The car overturned, finally rolling upright and coming to a stop. There was some damage to the car but the fan belt was still in working condition, so I drove the rest of the way and parked it behind the bus station.

In the morning, I went with my brother, Frank, to check it out and we noticed that the front window had been smashed. My brother couldn't believe that I survived the crash, thinking that I was thrown through the window. He gave me a slap on the back. I tried to explain to him that the window was fine when I left it but later found out that the bus drivers broke it in order to move my vehicle so they could get their busses out of the garage. Deciding that the car was jinxed; I sold it to a nearby garage mechanic.

I was always able to find work. I liked my work at a local gas station that paid me fifteen dollars a week. Back then that was a lot of money for pumping gas, changing oil, taking pump readings, and ordering supplies. One of the automobiles I was working on rolled away with me in it. The foot brake didn't work but I didn't realize it at the time. There was no note of bad brakes. The car and me landed on top of a pile of coal with all four wheels off he ground. I locked up the gas station and went to find two of my brothers for help. In a way it was a blessing in disguise that the coal was nearby or the car would have rolled over the creek bank.

I also had another job working nights in a bowling alley stacking pins. You would think it would be a safe job. While picking up the pins, some drunk threw his ball and it hit me in the head. I picked up the ball and sent it back, got dizzy and keeled over. The owners got scared and gave me a job as headwaiter. If it wasn't for a heavy crop of hair and a hard head I could have been killed. Once more I survived.

I really didn't like it so I quit this job and went to work in the canning factory in Angola. It's where my mother had worked at one time stirring tomato puree in two thousand-gallon barrels. My job was to sit on a platform between to large vats and keep the paddles turning the sauce while it cooked. It was hot work and if I felt weak I could easily fall into the sauce and no one would have know. My other duty was to check the gas flames beneath the cooking vats. This was another hot and dangerous place to be. I wasn't cut out for that line of work since I lost ten pounds in only three days, so I quit.

One of my buddies found me a job in a barrel factory. The owner was a bald-headed German fellow who treated us like dirt. This was around the same time that Hitler was creating a stir in Germany. This person reminded me of the dictator – the way he would raise his arm and say one minute do a certain job then five minutes later, raising that left arm of his again and say, "Why are you here?" – and send you off to work at another station.

One day I had had it with his dictatorial habits and asked the other workers why did they put up with this man? I finally stood up to him, asking: "Are you nuts? Why do you treat us like you do? We are human being, not animals." He then proceeded to raise his arm in that all too familiar pose again, until my temper got the better of me, and I turned around and socked him in the jaw! Right after that I punched out on my time clock and told him: "My paycheck better be here tomorrow when I stop to pick it up." Sure enough, the check was there and I left. I was told later on that he became a changed man after that. I'm glad I was able to make a difference for the workers who stayed on.

During my last job in Angola, I tried my hand working for the New York Central railroad. It was hard work – getting paid only fifty-three cents an hour – but I held in there, working all summer and through the winter. One old timer got himself killed and shortly after that I came very close myself. That's when I thought it was time to move on and landed in Buffalo.

I found a job working for Bell Aircraft in their lumberyard. My boss was very helpful; he taught me the ropes. I would also work the jackhammer and as a small tool repair operator. At this time they were taking stationary engineers into service so I was trained to take over some of their duties. One day I had to climb over a closed section to see what was wrong with the blower anchored above that department. I remember falling between two rafters, holding on for dear life. When suddenly four soldiers appeared with guns pointing at me. Talk about being scared out of my wits! I had apparently fallen into a classified "secret" department. The war had started and folks were on edge. I was offered a deferment from the draft due to the job I had at Bell, but I told them 'no', I wanted to join. I entered the service on August 31, 1943.

One of my co-workers, Joe Provino's wife, Phyllis, promised to write to me while I was in service. Many young men like myself were enlisting. I met two who only lived a block away from me and we all became fast friends by the time we arrived in New York City's Grand Central Station.

Chapter Three
My Military Life

The discipline had already started and we hadn't reported to basic training. An Army officer told us all to meet at a certain spot in New York City's Grand Central Station. . I had to go to the bathroom so I was a couple of minutes late. The Army officer started to dress me down. "You were suppose to be here two minutes ago."

I said that I was but didn't know how to get down here. My new friend, Tom, who became a lifetime friend, thought the officer was going to give me a hard time. We were all unsure what to expect. Fortunately, we never saw him again.

On the train, I was talking about my days panning for gold in the Klondike. I never was in Alaska and no one doubted my story. I don't recall how many days we stayed in Camp Upton. All the soldiers in my barracks got details until we were ready to ship out. I never got any detail assigned. A sergeant in charge of us said that there was a high-ranking soldier who had my same last name. Apparently, his name was helping me stay stateside under some protection. I never said a word; I just kept my mouth shut. To this day, I don't know who he was.

I don't recall what day we left Camp Upton, and no one knew where we were going. We were packed like sardines. I slept on a baggage rack the first night. I believe the first stop was the Harrisburg, Pennsylvania train yard. A work train with all woman workers on board was parked at the siding. Some of the soldiers jumped off the train and had a quick one. After that, there were new rules. At each stop all the doors were secured, no one got on or off.

We arrived at Camp Gruber in Oklahoma. With two heavy bags, it seemed like we were walking forever. I thought I wasn't going to make it. The two bags weighed more than me. I was now a soldier of the 42nd Rainbow Division infantry. We met our First Sergeant, a hard-faced older soldier who had been in the Army many, many years, who never smiled and never said much --- when he did, it was law!

Our first 30 days were confined to company area for short arm inspection. All we wore were the plastic raincoats in the scorching heat. Every time you moved you would get burned. When Mrs. Eleanor Roosevelt visited, we had to pass on parade in full field packs in 110-degree weather. Some soldiers were passing out.

During a night march in freezing weather, a soldier sat up in a tree and dropped his rifle. It hit me in the head and as I passed under the tree. I don't know if he did it on purpose or if it was just the extreme cold and he couldn't hang onto his rifle. He didn't come down from the tree so we could see who he was. When we got to the briefing room, the officer saw frozen blood on my head and neck.

I had a mild problem with the First Sergeant. I had problems with my shoes. The First Sergeant told me to take a shower with my shoes on and leave them on so they will dry and fit me better. That's what I did. When I didn't fall out for retreat, the top Sergeant came looking for me and found me taking a shower with my shoes on. For punishment, the top Sergeant gave me extra duty in the Supply Room after chow. When Captain Dye saw me, he asked me what had I done. I explained what happened. The Captain had a little grin and told the First Sergeant: "Give this soldier a three-day pass. This soldier obeyed your order."

I wrote my brother for some money. My answer: he was being drafted and couldn't send me any. I stayed three days in company area and had to hide every time I saw the First Sergeant. If he caught me in camp doing nothing, I would get a work detail. If you smoked and threw a butt on the ground, you would dig a six-foot hole, bury it, then dig it up again and put it in the right place. I tried to enjoy my three days.

Being confined to the PX in your area gave little for the men to do. The PX was always packed especially when this beautiful redhead was on duty. Not able to get to the counter, I asked one of the soldiers what her name was. So the next night, I called out: "Rose, your brother is here." Everyone turned to see who I was and moved to the side so she could see me. She looked at me. It was the most beautiful smile I ever saw.

"Brother, when did you get in? Mother didn't say anything." And then she hugged me when I got to the counter.

Boy, was I surprised. She didn't give me away. I never had to buy a drink when she was on duty. We played the game until I shipped out.

I found that I was a bit more naïve than I thought. The second month of being a soldier, I met another interesting woman on base. She wanted to know who i was. She told the First Sergeant that I looked like someone she knew. An orderly was sent to get me. We talked and then went in the PX. She had a Coke and I had a beer. She said I looked somewhat like her late husband. She showed me a picture of her late husband and there was some resemblance. One Sunday, I had a pass and she was there. She seemed to know when I was off duty. We went to her 2,500-acre horse ranch in her Caddy. When I got back to camp the First Sergeant wanted to see me. He wanted to know what was up.

I said, "Sarge, I am puzzled also. There was no kissing or sex, more like a brother and sister talking."

The Sergeant said, "She is playing it and trying to rope you in with her ranch and horses. She will tell you that this could all be yours. It's good that you are using your head. Some women are looking to marry a service man. If they get killed in the line of duty, they get the serviceman's insurance, and in the meantime, she can get the monthly checks. If he makes it back, she will divorce."

I asked the First Sergeant to tell her I am on duty if she comes by. I don't know what he told her; I never saw her again.

Receiving a weekend pass is what all the soldiers look forward to. One weekend my buddy and me decided to stay overnight, sleep in a good bed and get away from the Army cots. The innkeeper kept knocking on the door all night. She said she was concerned about the open gas heater. Finally, on her last attempt, my friend told her: "We are not gay and we will turn the heater off unless you want to come in also. So don't bother us again so we can get a good night sleep in a good bed."

In the morning, we went out to breakfast for ham and eggs and good coffee. It sure was better than Army chow. We hung around town for awhile and stopped at a tavern to have a beer. The redheaded girl that worked at the PX saw me come in. She was sitting with a sergeant. She got up and told him: "My brother has just come in. I will have to leave."

"It's all right," I said. "We're on our way back to camp."

"Next time you get a pass we all can have dinner with Mother."

She was still playing our game. This all happened shortly before shipping out. We left camp to go overseas and never got a chance to say goodbye.

As acting Sergeant, I was responsible for a platoon of soldiers. Once a week we would hike for five miles. Two of the forty-year-old individuals were not fit for duty and felt sorry for them. The older of the two was a Harvard professor and the other a tailor. It was very difficult to stay in line and they kept falling out of the march. The battalion colonel drove up to me in his Jeep, yelling, "Shorty, keep those men in line!" I did my best but it still didn't help. I explained to them that the Colonel was on my back. By this time, the Colonel was really pissed off and turned to me, saying: "You, Wop. I told you to get those men in line."

I then called the platoon to a halt, turned to the Colonel, saluting him and said, "Sir, my name is not Wop," in the loudest voice I could muster so the whole platoon could hear me. "If you don't know my name, it is Soldier, sir. You are about their same age. They never did any walking before, perhaps you can march with them to show them it can be done. I, for one, don't have my men do anything that I can't do myself."

"You're out of order."

I saluted and gave the command to march. I then got a Jeep to pick up the two soldiers. I was surprised the Colonel didn't come back.

Back at camp, I went to the Captain and explained the situation. "I want to bring the Colonel up on charges for calling me a Wop."

"The Colonel would have to sign papers to bring charges against himself. He won't do that," the Captain said, "because he knows you stopped the whole platoon to hear you saying that you didn't like being called a Wop."

I was told that the Colonel said I had spunk and there were no corporal stripes or sergeant stripes.

There was one soldier, not a teenager like the rest of us, about twenty-five with Coca-Cola glasses, real thick lenses, who was not picked to go overseas. Some of the soldiers told him so. I said that it's his glasses that are keeping him stateside. He resented me mentioning that it was his glasses and came to me where I was sitting on my top bunk and he started raising his voice. He had a loud voice, and he wanted everyone to pay attention to our confrontation. I told him, "You got me shaking in my boots. Go back to your cot before you get hurt. You won't get the Purple Heart and you will land in the hospital if you mess with me. It's not your fault if you're not picked. So thank your lucky stars and relax."

No more was said.

About two weeks later, the company started to pick soldiers to go overseas for front line duty. We were sent to a camp near the town of Baltimore, Maryland. Two other soldiers and me got a pass to Baltimore. One soldier, a former New York taxi driver, had the gift of gab. At a tavern, he noticed the tavern owner had pictures of race horses on his wall. The soldier got the tavern owner's ear. He said I was a jockey out of Fort Erie, New York near Buffalo. Now at that time you couldn't buy liquid in this town. He talked to the owner to sell us three bottles. We had met three girls in a lunchroom and had dates for later that night. The former taxi driver's wife was coming to meet him. He was worried that he had the clap. We said just use a condom. So he shows up with is wife and that was the end of our dates with two bottles of booze. We knew we could not pass by the MP gate with them, and we were not going to give them the booze so we emptied the bottles without getting a taste.

We left Baltimore and went to Norfolk, Virginia, awaiting our orders to board the Liberty Ship. To fill time, a bunch of us started talking about our younger days. When I was about 15, on weekends, I would bicycle to a small town about five miles away to work on this farm picking strawberries and chopping wood. I was told I would be working with the framer's sister who was seventeen and out of the Good Shepherd's Home. In the summer months I slept in a car and in the winter months I slept in the sun porch. One end of the porch faced the girl's bedroom window and the other end faced her brother's bedroom window.

One night as I was about to fall asleep, I got a lot of light at my end of the porch. I turned to see where the light was coming from. She was standing stark naked on her side of the window. She was ready to raise the window to come through. This scared the hell out of me. I grabbed my blanket and went to the other end of the porch. This girl was nuts. In the morning, I told the brother I was going back home. I didn't feel well. I knew that if I stayed there I would not survive. The brother would have killed me. I was told later that she would sneak out and go to town to get her kicks. If this was true or not, I didn't know or care. Story time was over. Orders came to board the Liberty Ship. I don't recall the ship's name. We were told that chocolate was a good item to have. Aboard ship, I went and sat on the anchor on the bow of the ship and felt each dip while eating my candy bars. I soon realized I was getting seasick. I was sick for three days and many more than that. The johns were all being used. With each dip of the ship, the john deck had become so slippery from puke that you would slide and puke over the other soldiers who were sitting on the johns.

I believe the bunks were stacked six high and I had the top bunk, a good place to be if someone got sick. I believe the convoy to Naples, Italy, sailed 28 days due to zigzagging to avoid U-boats. With 500 soldiers onboard, the chow lines were often long. A buddy and me set up a plan to get ahead of the chow line or at least up closer. With our life jackets on we would pretend to fight by punching each other, eventually getting to the head of the line and making our peace. This lasted about a week before the soldiers caught on.

Later, I got in good with a Navy sailor who did the baking and I would meet him each night and get fresh bread.

Off the coast of Algiers, April 11, 1944, on my mother's birthday, we were attacked by German aircraft. I was lying under the big gun when it was fired without warning. I felt like my brains were blown out and I still have trouble with my ear to this day. The loudspeaker announced that all Army machine gunners had to report to the gun decks, all others get below deck. The stairway to the above deck was loaded with soldiers waiting to be first to get out in case we got hit --- and 500 more to follow. If we got hit or sunk, we would die like rats. When we got the "all clear" signal the area we were at was riddle with bullet holes. We named the attack The Battle of the Garbage Cans because all the cans were shot up. Two of our army gunners were credited for shooting a German aircraft down. By the grace of God no one was hurt.

The ship was full of interesting soldiers, each with a story to tell. One American soldier, who sang love songs, had a beautiful voice. His voice reached each one of us. We heard that just before we landed at Naples, he had a heart attack. The last news we heard was that we would be flown back to the States.

We had another soldier who did nothing but brag about what he would do to the Germans. He would walk around the deck with his shirt off, showing his hairy chest and muscles. An hour or so before we were going to dock, he had all kinds of health problems: his stomach hurt, had chest and back pains, and headaches. He was rushed to a hospital. There was nothing wrong with him; he just turned out to be coward. Like I told my buddy, Tony, that he was just a blow hard, lot of wind and no guts. I don't recall what happened to him.

There was one soldier I am glad I was his friend, not his enemy. He was strong as a bull. He could put beer caps between all of his fingers and bend them in half at the same time. Some men could bend one cap between thumb and forefinger but not all the fingers at the same time. Incredible. He was a very quiet soldier. Didn't talk much. We were talking about how tough the skin of his hands were. One soldier, being funny, said to him, "Hey, can you put Tony's cigar out without burning yourself." My buddy, took the challenge and said to me, " Tony, bite on your cigar hard." Before I knew what happened, he ground my cigar right down to nothing. It's a good thing he told me to bite on the cigar or I could have choked to death. His hand was not burned.

I had a buddy named Deetz, a tall, quiet guy who was an artist. He could paint your picture better than a camera. A couple of guys picked on him and I would defend him. He had a mean, drinking stepfather who more or less put him in a shell and scarred him. He had two pictures in his wallet: his girl and his mother. His mother came to visit him in Oklahoma after basic. She was a large woman with one leg shorter than the other. She had a shoe that was a good six inches bigger than the other shoe. She thanked me for looking after him. Onboard ship, they made Deetz a "salt water non-com". You held this rank only when you were onboard. This helped to keep order while at sea. I got a letter from my mother that said when we got back to the States I was supposed to bring him home for an Italian dinner. Somewhere, in all of my letters from my mother, I still have that letter. I never got a chance to show it to him. We were separated to different companies. I was told that he was shot the first day of combat and killed. I wish I had been there when his mother got the news. She was not a well woman. I never got his mother's address; I wish I had.

When we landed in Naples, we met a lot of Italian kids with hands out. We were moved out fast. I don't know where we were sent. It was not too far from the front line. But first, we were sent to get some training by soldiers who had already seen combat, and then given malaria pills. Some of the soldiers had taken so many that they were turning green. I believe that's one of the causes of servicemen having spleen, liver and stomach problems today.

We were trained how to shoot a 30-caliber machine gun from the hip without a tripod, in case you had to fight house to house. One training soldier with greenish skin who saw too much combat was a very good for us. He received a "Dear John" letter that he was a proud father. He had been overseas for over a year. He shot himself. This soldier should have been sent home when he was no longer good for combat.

Not far from the frontline, we held regular marches to keep ready. One day, every soldier in camp had to go on a march. After an hour of marching, my buddy, Tony, who trained with me in the States, decided when we had a chance we would duck out and get back when they marched back. We came to a bend in the road and a big open gate centered in a high wall over a block long. When we entered we noticed these walls were graves. We didn't know this was a graveyard. There were rows and rows of walls of graves plus a few chapels with small altars.

Tony called me and asked, "How do you spell your last name?"

I said, "That's not funny."

"Come here, you have a relative here."

I walked to where Tony was and saw a nice altar and turned to see where he was pointing. About five feet above the floor I saw a picture of a bald headed man with a big mustache. It had to be a picture of my grandfather or my great, great grandfather. I wrote Mother a letter about it but it was censored.

We heard some noise that came from the basement of this building near a chapel. We spotted a grate on the floor. We raised the grate and saw steps going down and the noise got louder. I said that sounds like rats then we saw one that was at least a foot long. We dropped the grate and with no ammo for our rifles, we got the hell out of there. We hid outside the wall until our marching column came back. We slipped into the end of the column; we were never missed.

In our eight-man tent, while wanting for orders to move to the front, there were three older married men that didn't know what to write to their wives now that they were overseas. So I started to write their letters and for them to copy it and send them on. They were grateful to me but were surprised that I had such knowledge. I met two of the soldiers a couple of months later and the wives never realized how much the spouses felt toward them.

A short distance from the frontline, we were outside on the latrine when we heard the whistle of a bomb. We hit the deck with our pants down. If you don't hear the whistle, it's too late. As I look back on my life --- being on the frontline, not knowing what lay ahead for me, being told that I received last rites, saved from being run over by a streetcar, almost killed by a drunk knife-wielding Indian --- I just made up my mind that whatever came my way I would meet head on and survive.

A voice called out: "Get your gear. We're off to the front."

We were all ordered to get rid of all of our cigarettes and tobacco, and to put them in that room. You could not walk into this room; it was packed six feet high. At twenty dollars a carton, someone was going to make a bundle in the black market.

On May 12th, we reached the frontline. I asked the rest of the soldiers if they had any ammo. I said that if we get attacked, we are sitting ducks. I got the Sergeant and asked: "Where is the ammo dump? None of us have any ammo." The Sergeant got us the ammo. I picked up two bandoleers for over my shoulder, a .45 pistol, three hand grenades and two smoke grenades, ammo for my cartridge belt and pistol, and four clips for the BAR rifle. I was now ready. We were led into a big German hole in the mountain that you could hide a truck in. Being shelled all night and our machine guns firing all night, we didn't get much sleep. The ammo bearer constantly brought us ammo.

A First Lieutenant came to me from Headquarters Company and said he needed a soldier to read Italian maps and translate them. He asked me if I could read and speak Italian. I said I was sorry; I didn't understand or speak it. I lost out on a good position in Headquarters Company.

After all night fighting, we were off to fight another battle on another mountaintop. Donkeys were added to our column to bring much needed ammo. On the trail, the top of one of my grenades came off. Quick as a flash, I kicked it over the mountainside; nothing happened. "What a relief," the Sergeant smiled at me. "For it to go off, the pin has to be pulled. You're a good soldier to have with me."

We came under heavy fire, hitting the deck and crawling forward a few yards. The bullets were very close. You could hear them flying past you, some hitting the dirt around you. Still crawling forward as low as I could, I saw a soldier about twenty feet ahead of me. I called to him. "Can you see anything from your position?" No answer. I called him again. I kept crawling forward until I got next to him. I said, "We are all scared but we still got to go forward." I got closer to him. He had been dead for a couple of days. His body was decomposing with insects crawling out of his torn purple flesh – a sight I will never forget. This shook me up. I got up and ran forward toward a brick wall twenty feet ahead of me. The bullets were too close; they were passing all around me. I got behind the brick wall and hearing the bullets, I knew I had to get out of there. I was their target and the whole German army was firing after me.

Lucky for me, the wall curved down and away where I could stand up and jump down the mountainside. I landed on my left ankle and sprained it. I fell on my left shoulder and got a sharp pain radiating down my back. I crawled forward until a medic could get to me. He wrapped my sprain but could do nothing for my upper back. Every few days my ankle would be rewrapped. With the help of the medic, I went on chasing the Germans for seventeen more days on a sprained ankle.

We got orders to dig in. Heavy artillery fire was coming in. German tanks were not too far away, shelling went on all night. When morning came we were smack in the middle of a minefield. I had six mines around me. I called out that we were in the middle of a minefield. Eleven others and me had a big problem: how to get out of there without anyone getting hurt. Thanks to the Lord, none of us got hurt. I don't know what scared me more: being targeted by a bullet or being in a minefield. It's up to you, and only you, to get out of a minefield --- and the will of God --- and hope no one panics.

We got new orders to relieve the soldiers on the other side of another mountaintop and to carry five gallons of water on our backs, and then follow up on line in support of the soldiers that were fighting. You guessed it, I got the five gallons to carry, sprained ankle and all. The soldier in front of me carried my rifle and the soldier behind me was a BAR man. Every other soldier carried five gallons of water. Dog tired. Water was delivered and each man went right into the fighting, attacking the Germans. The Germans surrendered.

Later, we were off to climb another high mountain ridge with a very sharp drop facing the sea. We were told that the Germans might try to come that way and outflank us. The enemy's big guns were firing all night. We dug in about every twenty feet along the high ridge. German shells were not landing in our area. By the next morning, less than fifteen hundred feet away from us, we heard a lot of crying and screaming. When we climbed this mountain there was no one in sight. I started out to see where the crying was coming from. I saw the tall grass move about seventy-five feet in front of me. I put a shot near the spot where the grass was moving.

An Italian man jumped up with his hands up in the air. "Don't shoot", he said.

"You understand English?"

He nodded.

"Turn around and walk backward to me. Why are you crawling in the grass and where is all the crying coming from?"

"German shells killed two of our friends."

I told the nearest soldier to me, "I'm going to where he came from. Let the rest of the men know. If I don't come back, check it out."

I looked at the Italian man. "I don't see any homes. Where do your people live?"

"On the mountain," he said, pointing. I followed him.

Inside straw huts next to the mountain, there were a few men and women and their children, some young ladies, one a redhead. "Keep the women quiet or the Germans will zero in on you," I told them.

Some of them were eating polenta, a mixture of goat's milk and cornmeal. I was offered some. I told them, "You to eat it first."

The man insisted that I eat first. I pulled out my .45 and said, "You and the redhead eat first. If you get sick I will shoot both of you."

They ate. Nothing happened. I didn't eat any because it was mixed with goat's milk. I went back to my squad and asked the men if they wanted some Italian polenta. I went over with each soldier that wanted some, and in turn, they left some of their rations, mostly chocolate.

The German's big guns started firing again. Back at my foxhole, I noticed the redhead coming to find me. She was scared stiff and stayed in my foxhole all night. I handed her my prayer book and read some passages to her. She understood

English. She would say in her soft voice, "Tony, rest. I will watch."

I didn't understand how they lived on top of a mountain in straw huts and be able to understand English. I never got around to ask her. In the morning, the Sergeant said we were moving out. We had to climb this mountain to see from where the Germans were shelling. The redhead stayed by me, climbing with me for the next three hours, offering me goat's milk that she carried. She kept insisting, telling me that the goat's milk would pick me up. I hated goat's milk.

We were all dog-tired, so tired that it was an effort to raise your feet. My left ankle was killing me and my back was sore. I never said a word. We were told the Germans were fighting in the village just over this ridge. As soon as we were told that the Germans were near, it was like we got a shot of something. All the tiredness just left. I told the girl she had to leave. She said she wanted to fight with us.

"Go to your people and tell them there won't be any more shells in your area."

We moved on, over the top right into action. The Germans were caught off guard. They didn't expect to see Americans coming over this mountaintop. After a very short battle, some ran, the rest surrendered. More days of fighting, more mountains to climb, and my left ankle was and leg and upper back were killing me. I never complained. There was a battle I had to finish. I don't recall the redhead's name. I wanted to go back to tell her I was all right. I didn't even recall where the area was.

On a hard climb to another mountaintop, a big Italian with gold teeth said he was in America, made his money and moved back to Italy. He then said, "You are Italian and a traitor, coming here, shooting Italians." He raised his hand as if to strike with the backside of his hand.

"You son of a bitch," I said, and struck him with the butt of my rifle. "We came to save your ass. We are all tired of climbing these mountaintops here, you ungrateful bastard."

Being shelled, we had to see who was directing the enemy fire. Sgt. Bouchard and me and another soldier went out on patrol. We spotted a house in a valley where it had a view of the mountainside and could direct fire on us. It had taken quite awhile for us to get there without being spotted. Before the house, there was an outpost of three German soldiers as lookout. We waited until it got dark to dispatch the others. I have a German flag and bayonet as a souvenir. The house was destroyed.

Marching down this road with a big open field ahead, a cliff to the left, and a forest to the right, would be a good place for

Germans to hide and attack. When we got in the middle, the Sergeant said, "I'm going to send a soldier to that cliff so he can see what's in the valley ahead of us."

Without a word, I was off to the top of that cliff on the curve of the road. I figured that once I got up there, I could rest until the company got there. I was lucky one more time. As I got up on that cliff, there was a big boulder that I could get behind and look all over the valley. Just as I got behind the boulder, bullets were bouncing off the boulder. I was now in a very bad spot, all by myself. The Sergeant was too far in the rear. The sniper, keeping me busy, had to be in the forest. I didn't know if he could move to get into a better position to take a shot at me. I started to crawl deeper behind the boulder. I was lucky the ground sloped downward. I threw rocks near the entrance so he would think I was still there.

I made up my mind that the bullet was not going to have my name on it. I knew if I got up to jump down the cliff, I would be a dead duck, so I started crawling down the slope to see where it was going. It seemed to be going down to the other side, away from the German view. I crawled as far as I could. I put the helmet strap under my chin and my rifle tight to my body then somersaulted down the mountainside --- hitting every rock with my bad left leg and my upper back. I could hear a lot of gunfire. I knew the Sergeant and his men were in trouble. Once I got to the bottom, I was lucky one more time. I landed in a low area and the road had a high shoulder. I crawled below the high shoulder without being noticed. I crawled very slowly so I wouldn't make any dust. I got within seventy-five feet of the Sergeant but he was on the other side of the road in some kind of ditch, but not in a position to see where the Germans were.

I yelled out, "They are firing from the trees in the rear. They let you pass."

I don't know how long I lay there. There was a bush about ten feet ahead of me. Once I made it to the bush, I tried to talk to the Sergeant but I didn't know if my voice would carry across too far, from the road to the trees.

"If I see one. I will take a shot. It's about three or four hundred yards. I got him in my sight," and I took a deep breath and squeezed the trigger. I could see him raise up and fall. I believe it was a shoulder shot. I got to the Sarge and said, "They are snipers with a machine gun, otherwise they would have attacked."

We took a short break. The Sarge decided to read a letter from his wife, telling him how tough it was in the States, that they had to eat cold cuts. He got so pissed he passed it on to each of us. "When I say 'go', get your ass up and move," he growled.

We crossed that open field and you could hear the bullets zipping through the grass. By the grace of God, we made it. We were now at the bottom of the forest tree line. As we scanned the area, the BAR man let out a burst of gunfire into the trees. A German came out with his hands on his head and walked to me. I told him to stop. He was about ten feet from me, clean uniform and shined boots. He said in very good English: "You Americans can't shoot straight. You Americans got so much ammo that we have to surrender."

"You're lucky that we can't shoot straight," I said. "You will be able to go home." I turned him over to the BAR soldier to bring him back to Headquarters. I had enough problems going forward, I wasn't going to walk him to Headquarters.

On high ground, we spotted four German tanks next to a mountainside where Americans couldn't spot them until it was too late. The Sarge called in its position. We moved back about two hundred yards. Within five minutes there were no more tanks.

I don't recall when we were ordered to get rid of our gas masks and put hand grenades in the gas mask holder. We were also ordered to fix bayonets for our next attack.

We were short of water and there was a well in a little gully. We were told if we went to the well without weapons the Germans wouldn't shoot at us, and in turn, we would not shoot at the Germans. It was our turn to go to the well. I went to the well with four canteens. I noticed four Italian women at the well all dressed in black getting water. Four American soldiers stood at the well talking filthy to them. The women were smiling but didn't understand them. When I got to them, they tried to speak to me. I told them the soldiers were crazy. I then turned around and laid into them, "How would you like it if these ladies were your mother or sister --- and jerks like you were talking like you are doing. You would knock the hell out of them. Get your water and go or I will turn you over to your Captain."

One lady pointed her finger at the soldiers and spit on the ground; the ladies dropped their buckets. And then I began filling my canteens and they gave me the sign of the cross. I thanked them and offered them something out of my K rations. If it was true or not about the Germans not shooting, all I know was that no shots were fired.

Our company was ordered for R and R, rest and relaxation. The Germans were on the retreat after being on line for a long time. The 92nd Division would be taking our position. The doctor said, "We will be on R and R for two weeks and I want you off your feet. If you need anything the Sarge will see to your needs.

After two days in the rest area, the doctor wanted to see me. He said, "I'm sorry but your outfit was called back up. The Germans are making a stand and the 92nd needs help. However, I'm sending you to the hospital. You've been on that ankle close to three weeks and it's three times larger than a normal ankle. I don't know how you did it. The First Sergeant offered you rides when available and you refused them."

While being processed for the hospital in the rear area, a shot rang out. One of the soldiers still had a bullet in his rifle. It just missed my head and the medic's head. Another close call. I was sent to a hospital above Naples. There was no room in that hospital so the first night we slept outside on hospital grounds. Sleeping or half asleep, I don't know, I felt something on my leg. I jumped and grabbed it and threw it as hard as I could. It hit the flagpole and I heard the scream of a cat. I limped to the flagpole to see if the cat was okay; the cat was gone. An orderly came over to see what happened. I told him about the cat and that I was okay.

The second night in the hospital, the Colonel, who was head nurse, came to my bedside and said, "Your records state you are type O positive. We have a soldier who has his leg amputated and needs blood.

I just said, "Let's go," and started to get out of bed.

The nurse Colonel Shepherd said, "Wait, we will get a wheelchair." A bed was set up next to the soldier and a unit of blood was transferred from me to the wounded man. I wonder where this soldier is and if he knows that he has Italian blood in his body.

In the hospital, I met a young Italian boy who worked in the hospital. He spoke perfect English. Whenever he had time he was at my side. He was like a younger brother that I had at home. I promised to keep in touch with him when I got out of the service. I feel really bad at eighty years old. I still think of him. He wanted to go to America. I hope he made it.

Two days after being in the hospital, I dropped a card to my sergeant and in a few days I received a card back… and across it was the word: deceased. I was wondering if his wife wrote him another letter, stating how tough she had it or a "Dear John" letter. I was told he charged a tank with a .45 handgun. I felt bad that I wasn't there. When he needed help, I might have been able to calm him down.

Four Red Cross nurses worked in the hospital. They were all great. There was one who worked our ward passing out items that the soldiers might need or writing letters for them. All the guys went ape every time she came through. She was about five foot eight, a beautiful build, brown hair with a gray streak, and about 30 years old.

When she came through the ward, I paid no attention to her. I watched Vivian for a couple of days and saw she was really concerned about the soldiers; it was not just a job to her. The soldiers asked me why I wasn't paying any attention. She was beautiful – a breath of fresh air. I figured that if I acted like the others, I would be just another soldier.

One day she sat on my bed and asked me, "What is your name and how is your leg doing? Is it any better?"

Just small talk. Every day after that she passed out her items then she would sit on my bed. She wanted to know if she could write letters to my mother or my girl. She'd say: "I see you have no writing paper or a pen." Little by little, I had all of her attention.

When I could get around a little better, Vivian asked me if I could help her pass out some of the items. She wanted me to be active. One day she said, "Tony, come to my office to pick up the items." A couple of soldiers said to me, "You are a smooth one. You pay no attention to her and now you got all her attention."

I was in her office every day, even after the items were passed out. There was a soldier patient who was an MP. He was tall, and looked somewhat like Cary Grant, and thought he was God's gift to women. One day he said to me: "I've been trying to get in her office for two weeks and you are there every day and sometimes all day. What's going on? What do you have that I don't have?"

"For one," I told him, "I'm not trying to get in her pants. You said 'I am short' and you 'are tall and handsome'. You look in the mirror all the time, telling yourself that you are handsome. What you see is just the outside skin. It's what's inside that counts. Also, short people can get in places where tall people can't. If you are done bragging about yourself, I have to go. My girl is expecting me."

As I got near her office, Vivian opened the door and said: "Tony, what's taking you so long?" and pulled me in, adding, "I was watching the two of you talking and could hear what you were talking about. I had the window open," she confided. "Look at him standing there. He is wondering what just happened. All the nurses are wise to him and he only wants one thing --- a push over to women. If he's smart, he would think over what you said; but I doubt it."

In our talks I told Vivian I had trouble sleeping nights. She said that if she could get me a job baking cookies, would I go for it? I had to agree. She talked to the full Colonel Shepherd and the job was mine. From noon on through the day I would help Vivian then from 10 p.m. to 3 a.m. I baked cookies. At 2 a.m., I would bring cookies to all the nurses on the floor; something they never had. When the doctors came to do their morning rounds, the female Colonel of nurses explained that I couldn't sleep nights and sleeping pills didn't work.

This went on for three months until I was transferred from the hospital. The Colonel of the nurses tried to have me transferred to their hospital, but the roster for transfers had been filled; it was too late. While I was baking cookies, something bit me on the left shoulder. The spot got as big as an egg. I was given a shot in my arm. I believe that's what gave me my spleen problem.

There was this beautiful blonde nurse who gave shots. One day she had to give a shot to a soldier who had VD She would slap the soldier on the butt and throw the needle like a dart. I was standing next to the Colonel's desk when this blonde nurse came up and said: "I don't know how that soldier got VD I've seen big ones and small ones but I never saw one that little." We all got a good laugh.

I was reclassified before I left the hospital. My leg wasn't in shape for front line duty. I said my good byes to the Italian boy, and to Vivian, the Red Cross nurse. She gave me her apartment address in case I was in the area. I thanked her for all the passes she got me so I could go to Naples, and for all the packages she sent to my mother under the Red Cross seal. The Americans were in good hands with Vivian. I visited Vivian once with another soldier. My dealings with Vivian were all above board and clean. She told me that the MP soldier never got in her office and never got a date with the nurses.

One hundred ex-combat soldiers were sent to Mussolini Racetrack. I was one of them; we were stationed there for eleven weeks. I swear we ate hash or SPAM for those eleven weeks and put on weight. I had a detail of soldiers doing yard work. This is where I met this American soldier who gave me his cousins address. He said she liked to kiss but not to tell her he told me this. I wrote to the girl and told her I would visit when I got to the States. Many letters were exchanged.

We were transferred again. One hundred ex-combat soldiers were sent to Caserta to be orderlies for the officers --- shine their shoes, make their beds, and so on. We were told that the Italians, who we replaced, were stealing their cigarettes. When we got there we were considered as a lot of bums and not liked by the rear echelon soldiers or officers, so after a couple of days we got fed up. After risking our lives, we were supposed to shine shoes.

One day we just didn't steal their smokes; we stole their whiskey. Not a shot or two, we stole the whole bottle. Not being a whiskey drinker, I didn't steal any whiskey because I'm a beer drinker. The rear echelon soldiers were on the first floor and the ex-combatants were on the second. The ex-coms were having a party with the stolen booze. It was getting loud, very noisy. A few from the downstairs came up the stairs but only to the landing, and said if we didn't shut up they were going to come up and teach us ex-coms a lesson. They figured we were a bunch of cripples and could handle us.

The soldiers went back down but not by the stairs. It seems that they missed all the stairs on the way down. I knew the fight was on its way, so I got on the top bunk to have a ringside seat. There were thirty of us ex-coms against them. They didn't have a chance. Those who did make it to the second floor landed in the hospital.

In the morning formation, the Colonel said, "What a sad looking bunch of bums." The Colonel was fit to be tied. As he walked down the ranks, he said to me, "What happened to you?"

"Nothing, sir."

"I can see that you are in perfect dress uniform. The rest, I don't know what they are. What happened last night?"

"I don't know, sir."

"What do you mean, 'you don't know'? You were there."

"Yes, sir. I was asleep."

"What do you mean 'asleep' with all that noise."

"Sir, in combat you learn to sleep with guns and cannons going on, so if there was a fight, it would be nothing... if there was a fight."

The colonel was really upset now. I then said, "Sir, we are combat men not orderlies to officers. This is a disgrace to all of us. We're all ready to give up our lives to shine shoes, I think not."

We were all transferred the same day.

I was put in charge of twenty Italian women cleaning up the castle in Caserta. I didn't mind this detail. All the women knew their jobs and did them well. I was talking to one of the Italian ladies, she asked me if she could get a pass to go to the town of Cassino to see if she could find her parents. The town had been leveled in a bombing raid. While I was talking to this young lady, an officer said: "WOP, get away from that girl. She needs something better than you."

I didn't move.

"Oh, you don't understand English. All WOPs are alike."

"You are out of order, you bastard. I am an American soldier and Italian, not a WOP. This lady understands English, and I want your name so I can press charges against you."

He left so fast, I thought he had wings. I never saw him again.

This young lady was now in charge of her section of the castle cleaning. Two other soldiers and me were transferred again to a town called Recal, Italy, about two miles from the Caserta Castle. My new outfit was the 849th Signal Intelligence unit. Here we were, down-graded again. Our job was to peel potatoes all day, day after day.

After the first day we refused to work. We told those who were in charge that we didn't have to pull any duty, so we just hung around to be discharged. The Colonel didn't like ex-coms coming into his outfit and sent us to the hospital to have our heads examined. We met an ex-combat doctor who held the rank of major --- our first break. We told the doctor what was going on with us and other combat men that left the combat area. We told the major that we didn't mind doing our share but that we didn't like being downgraded. I told him I had knowledge of running a PX and a movie projector. The other two said they would pull front guard duty.

With the doctor's orders, we got the jobs. I replaced the soldier at the PX and he was sent out for combat training. He sure was pissed. I ran movies three times a week.

We had a First Lieutenant, often called an LT, who was in charge of the PX. He had a weird sense of humor and didn't like ex-combat soldiers. He also thought it was funny by going behind a soldier and poking him or "goosing" him when he wasn't expecting it. He thought it was funny to see a fellow jump.

It was announced that when the ex-coms arrived, do not approach them from the rear, you could be attacked and hurt real bad. I told my partner, "When we loaded the truck, and when I am bending over and the LT is about to goose me, cough." I knew that my position while bending over would be too much for him to resist. I heard the cough and just as he touched me, I turned and slugged him right across the chin. The LT fell and hit the villa wall. He was in bad shape. I jumped off the truck, bad leg and all, and went to see the Captain, who happened to be a doctor and an ex-com. I told him what happened. He lay me down on the table behind a curtain and gave me a shot to calm me down.

The Colonel came down with his Lieutenant. The LT ran to the Colonel instead of going directly to the doctor. The doctor did take care of the LT's face. Boy, did he have a bruise. The LT said to the Colonel: "I want a court martial against this soldier for striking an officer."

The doctor said to the Colonel: "There won't be any court martial against this soldier. He's lying down behind this curtain. I gave him a shot to calm him down. I believe it was you, sir, that warned the camp not to approach the combat men from the rear, and the LT was standing right by your side. The LT thinks it's funny to go around goosing the soldiers because he likes to see them jump. It was just a matter of time before someone nailed him. He also degrades the Sergeant when the Sergeant has a detail of men picking up butts. He tells the Sergeant to pick them up, too. If there is any court martial, it will be against the LT."

The LT was transferred. I found out that all officers were being wise in rank except the doctor. Because he was a combat doctor, he felt it was held against him. His words, not mine.

One day, we had to bring supplies to a German prisoner of war camp and there was that LT that I socked. He was in charge of the mess hall, overseeing the Germans serving the food. He was in the far corner. I guess being a Jew and knowing Germans hated Jews, he kept his distance. There was better food in the German mess hall than in ours. When I handed my plate over to be served, the German put a small portion on it. I grabbed a knife and leaned toward him and said "more", and more I got. I guess he thought short men didn't eat much.

Back at camp with the 849th, I had it made working in the PX and showing the movies three times a week. When USO shows came over to perform, I helped to set up the stage. I got to meet the movie stars. Most of the stars hung out with the officers after the show. I only remember one group that hung out with the soldiers. In fact, this one group wanted us to drive them to their quarters. The names have vanished after so many, many years.

I was b.t.o. from e.t.o --- "big time operator" from "European Theater of Operation" --- and the Italian kids came to see all the movies. Some of the Italian workers, when they went back to their town, their kids would say: "Tony actor cinema." I had no problems when I went into their town. They thought I was a big shot in the States and spent a lot of time with Italian families.

I met a soldier who was with the 82nd Division, and he was now an MP. He gave me an MP armband. He would come by my camp and pick me up then go into the off limit areas checking to see if any soldiers were there and could be arrested.

There was only one Italian lady that I went out with who I could trust. I would leave my dog tags and clothes in her home and go to the beach that was off limits to servicemen. There was a long wooden walkway over the water with many small dressing huts. I was drying off her back when an MP came along and said to his buddy, "What is that short doing with that beautiful girl? What does she see in him?" The MP came close to us trying to make contact with her. She backed up and said, "Go fig your sister. I will tell your Captain."

He backed off. She grabbed my arm and I got in front of her. I stood there playing dumb. I wanted to hit him. If he found out I was a soldier, he would have grabbed me and put me in jail. Nothing came of it. We went back to her place and got in the tub to wash the salt off our bodies with our bathing suits on. There was no sex with this young lady. She made this clear on every date. She wanted to go to the United States with me. I would never marry any foreign lady. First, I was too young; second, was it love or stateside they wanted?

One day I was walking with an MP and there was a beautiful lady built like Sophia Loren sitting on her front step. She was well dressed. The MP went up to the step and asked her if she had any girls working. She got up and in plain English said, "This is not a whorehouse. How dare you, making such a statement. Who is your Captain?"

Her father and mother came out and wanted to know what was going on. "I am a doctor," he said, "and this is my daughter who is a nurse and waiting for me. You come here to insult her? Go or I will get in touch with your Captain."

Boy, am I glad I wasn't wearing the MP armband. On my next pass, I stopped at her home and talked to the young lady's father, and said I was sorry for the way the MP spoke to her. I asked the father if I could take his daughter to lunch and where was there a good place to have dinner, and dinner only. I asked the mother if she would like to go with us. We had dinner about once a month at her home.

That same MP buddy eventually married an Italian girl. When he parachuted, he had landed in her backyard. She hid him while the Germans were searching the area. When I had a pass, he would come to my camp and give me things to bring to her. This one day, he gave me five pounds of contraband sugar and I was hitch hiking to Naples. A First LT picked me up and offered to take me where I was going in order to give my leg a rest. Every so often he would look at me and smile with small talk. I was scared stiff. I was ready to throw it away if he asked me what was in the bag. I believe he knew I was nervous. As he dropped me off, he said to be careful with that bundle, and then smiled.

The day arrived when Ted, my long time Army friend, was to get married to the Italian lady who saved his life. He was late for his own wedding. Everyone was at the altar except the groom. The bride was getting nervous. The Best Man was there; everybody was there except the groom. Then here came Ted running down the side aisle. The wedding was great but I thought we were going to kneel all day. The wedding dinner was a seven-course meal. The last course was a big fish with the eyes still in its head. The reception was great, lots of dancing. The Italians and the soldiers mixed well. Lots of wine and singing and people feeling good.

I don't know why I asked one girl to dance with me because I didn't know how to dance. The girl said, "I don't dance with cripples."

The bride overheard what the girl said. The girl was a long-time friend of the bride. Then the bride said, "No one insults my husband's friends. If you can't be nice, the party is over for you."

I couldn't believe what I had just witnessed. I said, "It's all right; I don't even know how to dance. I should have never asked for a dance. I believe it's the wine."

My mother sent me a pair of nylons to give to the bride. She was so happy I thought I gave her a pot of gold. I still have the letter that she sent to my mother. The sad part of this is that after I was discharged, all contact was lost. Yesterday, I found Ted's Army serial number. I hope it's not too late. I would like to hear from him.

My buddy, Antonelli, an American soldier who spoke Italian very well, knew a family in town about a mile away. We decided to celebrate that the war was over. Everyone was celebrating. We drank wine all day. My friend had to go to the outhouse. About a half-hour later, the Italian host said, "I believe your friend fell in," and started to laugh.

I went to check on him and he was asleep on the john. I got him back to the house. Now it was my turn to use the john. My friend came looking for me. I was all right, I just couldn't get off the john because my feet didn't touch the floor, and I had drunk enough to say 'the heck with it', and just sat there. We both made it back to the house.

The lady of the house said, "What I have here is three happy drunks. I have the perfect drink for happy drunks --- Italian coffee. The next two hours, nothing but coffee, very strong coffee that would blow the top of your head off. She said: "Americans can't drink strong coffee."

I wanted to leave before dark. I didn't want to be hi-jacked before we got to camp. It was known that when Americans got drunk, they got robbed. We paid the lady what we owed her and a little extra, which she didn't want to take. About half way to camp, I told my friend that we were being followed. "They are hiding in a ditch about two hundred feet behind us. Walk slow. I am going to sit and take my Baretta from my holster. Then come and pick me up. They will think that we are really drunk."

We staggered more on purpose, our minds were clear; the coffee did the trick. We stopped like we couldn't move another step. That did it. They started to run toward us. When they got within fifty feet of us I turned and fired three shots at their feet. You never saw two men run away so fast in your life. We laughed all the way back to camp with no more problems. Italian coffee served its purpose.

The same buddy knew another family: four ladies in the fifty-five-year-old bracket. They served drinks to some servicemen. One lady, about forty-five, was cooking fry peppers. She was about five foot nine, and one hundred sixty-five pounds, a strong-built woman, who lost her husband in the war. She called me to the stove and said, "You no eat peppers in a long time. I have these peppers, Italian sausage, homemade bread and wine. Call your friend and sit with us over there and we will eat a good meal, a good change from Army food." We stayed awhile listening to Italian singing. I didn't understand the words but that didn't matter. The Italian songs were beautiful. We gave the ladies extra money and thanked them and left.

I remember one time, I went out alone looking for a relative many miles from camp and got lost. About 11:30 p.m. on a dark road, an Army truck passed me. I yelled, "Do you pick up American soldiers?" They stopped and delivered me to camp. I would have been AWOL if I hadn't been picked up.

I recall one day, Tony and I had a pass and went to Naples at our favorite café. It was run by a down to earth Italian family who loved Americans. As Tony and I were sitting at a table drinking, the owner's wife came to us and said that this Italian man didn't like Americans and he is bragging what he is going to do to Americans, so be careful.

This Italian started to our table, shouting that his girl went out with an American, and he was going to cut his throat. I reached for my Baretta and had it on my lap. When he was about a foot from our table, he had a knife in his hand, and as he raised it, I put a shot to the floor between his feet. It startled him and the knife came down into the table. I then put the gun to his head and told him to sit. Tony broke the knife. I called the owner's wife over and asked, "Does he speak English?"

"He understands good," she said.

"I am only going to tell him once. If you were a soldier in America, you would try to date American girls. Am I right?"

He agreed.

"You are lucky I didn't shoot you. Your girl left because you are nothing but a drunk and saw no future with you. We came here to save you from the Germans, and many Americans died to save your ass. I could turn you over to the Italian police but I am not."

The owner told him never to come in their place again.

On the way to Caserta Castle to pick up the movie reels, I would stop at this Italian lady's house and drop off our uniforms to be washed and pressed. This lady was a schoolteacher and she had two children: a boy and a girl. They all spoke English, except the teacher's mother. With the children in school and the grandmother in the kitchen, I was sitting in the living room sipping anisette that she gave me. The lady came to me and said that her mother is in the kitchen cooking. "Come we will sit down to eat while you wait for your clothes." This was the same day the peace treaty was being signed in this castle while I was picking up movie reels, and I didn't know it.

Getting ready to be shipped out back to the States, I had to order our last supplies for our camp. So on the inventory I had to put down how many soldiers were in camp. I figured the soldiers who were on detach service from our camp would be back so instead of ordering beer for two hundred, I ordered for four hundred. The supply was delivered. The soldiers and officers all got extra beer. I was told two days before we got shipped out that there was some question about inventory; nothing was said to me.

The ship that we sailed on to come home was a banana boat. Most of the men slept on the deck, no worry about German U-boats. This ship was loaded with soldiers and Army nurses. I ran the movies on the trip to the States and slept on the deck in the officer's quarters. We docked in Norfolk, Virginia. A band playing was playing as we got off the ship. A WAC greeted each soldier as they got off the ship. She looked at me twice and said, "Where did he come from?" I guess she was surprised to see a short soldier. I resented the remark at the time.

I was sent to Fort Monmount, New Jersey. I was put in charge of quarters --- CQ. I was on a pass and went to Raritan, New Jersey, to visit my Aunt Nellie and Uncle Devey, who had just got out of the service. He served in the Far East as a combat medic. Uncle Devey, Aunt Nellie, and three of her girl friends and me were at a nightclub. I was in full uniform with all my ribbons and medals, and the waitress would not serve me. She said I was too young. I said: "I just came from a war and you sure as hell will bring me a drink or you are going to have a war here."

Then my Uncle Devey spoke up, "He is old enough and you better serve him or there will be a war here and you will be out of a job!" She served us.

Uncle Devey and I went to a clothing store to buy him a suit. The sales person tried to sell him a purple suit. I blew my stack. Just because we were away in a war, we were not stupid or shell shocked. Don't try to push something that you can't get rid of. Uncle Devey never said a word and he got a beautiful

71

suit. I visited every lady who had written to me, so on another pass I went to Stoughton , Mass. She was the girl that her cousin had given me her address because she liked to kiss. She met me on a little bridge with her two younger brothers. I don't recall how I got from that bridge to the train. It was about a twenty-mile drive to her house. It was like a homecoming: the whole family was there, even the married sister and her husband. What a welcome! What a display of food!. My first home cooked American food in nearly three years. I couldn't believe my eyes. What a family! I felt like it was my family and my homecoming.

As we all sat down to eat, the married sister said: "Another WOP in the family." I believe that is what they wanted. That night that statement had me thinking. They just met me. Why did they want this girl married to someone they just met? In the morning, the father asked me to go in the cellar to show me his wine barrels, and to tell me about all the property he owned and how he wanted a son-in-law to run things with him until his sons could take over.

I didn't think too much about it at the time until later. I liked the family and wondered why they were pushing the girl on me. I had no feeling for this girl; I just wanted to visit and see who she was and thank her for writing.

We set a date for that night and she made a date the same night with another soldier, someone that she grew up with. Her father said, "Go out with Tony. He came a long way to see you, and go out with Jim when Tony leaves. She said, "No, I am going to have two soldiers tonight."

While sitting in the back seat, she chose to sit in the middle. She said, "It's all right with Tony."

I asked her, "What's okay with me?"

"It's tight back here and Jim wants to put his arm above me."

"Okay," I replied.

He was talking about when they were young, and how they hung their feet out of the window, letting me know he had the inside track. He was wasting his time because I wasn't interested in her. When I closed the window due to the rain, I could see in the glass that they were kissing and she was kissing back like they didn't know I was there. I could see now why the parents were acting like they did.

When we got back to the house, she jumped her two brothers for listening to Gangbusters on the radio. She seemed disturbed. I suppose she wished I wasn't there. I asked, "Why did you ask me if it was all right with me for Jim to put his arm around you. It's your shoulder, not mine."

She flew off the handle. "I don't want to go steady with any guy that knows what I'm going to do before I do it."

The statement didn't make any sense to me. I just dropped it, and she went to bed. I sure wouldn't be interested in a girl when she kisses another when your back is turned. What would she do when you are not around?

The next night we went to a show. I felt she didn't want to go. I put my arm on the back of the seat and it was put down for me. In the morning, I had to leave and go back to camp. The mother offered to drive me to the train and she came to the porch and waved as we were leaving. I wonder what she told her parents. When I got back to camp, I wrote her, thanking her for all the letters. I never heard from her.

At camp when I got of CQ duty, I went to the PX to get a chair so I could sit. This Italian prisoner of war, who was also called a "signee", pulled the chair from me and gave it to an American girl who was visiting him. I cracked him on the head with my cane then yelled out: "You combat soldiers! This prisoner of war grabbed my chair." That was enough. A fight started and the MPs came and were told what happened. The MPs beat the hell out of them and finished the job for us. In the morning back at CQ, the Captain said, "I hear there was a riot last night in the PX and a short American soldier was involved and the Italian prisoner lost. If I knew who he was, I'd give him a medal." He winked. He knew, and he knew I knew. This prisoner had full run of the PX, day and night. If you wanted to buy something it was already gone; the prisoner already bought it.

One day, I was in the hospital as a patient. Next bed to me was that Italian prisoner. American women were bringing in cakes and cookies and paid no attention to the American soldiers. The nurses didn't like it and said so. They laughed every time they came, looked at you, turn to the Italian and both laughed. When I left in full uniform with medals, I went to his bed and told his visitor, "This man shot at Americans and you visit a prisoner and not Americans." He was going to say something. I turned and said, "If you are at the PX, stay clear of me because you are going to be back in this hospital or the morgue." All the nurses clapped and I left.

I am now a civilian and thinking about when I was young and what I went through. In these past years, I was thinking about my friend Frank. We were sitting under a bridge, talking about the rise of Hitler and that when we got old enough, we would join. I wanted to be a gunner in an airplane. Frank wanted to be a machine gunner. Little did I realize that that day would come. My friend had very bad eyesight and the service would not take him. He felt very bad. I still couldn't believe that I was in the infantry. I should have been a gunner in an airplane. Then I was thinking about the present and I believe as an infantry soldier, I learned more about the people, the war, and my fellow soldiers as we went through town after town. The hardship endured by people and soldiers is something I will never forget. I doubted that I would have ever gotten this type of experience as an airplane gunner.

Still running things through my mind, I recall meeting the Pope as we were standing in front of the railing. The Pope would go to each soldier as he blessed them, and in turn, we would kiss his ring. He would mention which country you were from. The soldier standing next to me was black. The Pope said, "Africa."

The soldier replied very loudly, "American."

The Pope said, "Sorry." The Swiss Guards turned as the American spoke, "America."

My mind in now back with the 849th Signal outfit, after combat I met a soldier who was photographer for the 849th. He arranged to get a five-day pass to Rome for us. The deal was, he didn't have any money. I would pay for everything and I would get copies of all the pictures. Bat knew a family in Rome plus he spoke and understood Italian. It was a beautiful house and I had to go to the bathroom so I used the word that stateside Italians use in the streets but the lady didn't understand me. I grabbed my belt to let her know and she came out with the word 'gabinetto'. I said, "I don't want to go in your cupboard." We all had a good laugh. I came back and said, "Bat, there is no toilet in there, just a hole in the tile and two foot places." He took it in stride.

We took a whole bunch of pictures. My buddy, Bat, had photos of Mussolini hanging up-side-down. Bat gave me a lot of pictures of Mussolini to put in my footlocker that he was going to write about and put in a book. This one Major knew that Bat went to Rome with me. Knowing that Bat took photos, and after checking Bat's locker and finding nothing, he figured I might have them. He raided my footlocker and stole all the pictures. We later saw photos in Yank Magazine and knew they were Bat's pictures.

I believe the Major made some money on Bat's pictures. This Major really thought he was something. He had a trim moustache. If a GI was in town from our camp and with a girl, he would butt in and the GI would take a back seat. One day Bat and I were with two beautiful Italian ladies having a drink. Here comes the Major, trying to be one of the fellas. We were wise to him. As he came to our table, Bat said something to the girls in Italian. I told the Major that we wanted to be alone.

"No officers," the one lady said in English. "Get lost, Mr. Mustache."

Poor Major, his pride was hurt. A few days later while waiting to be moved out to a truck to catch a boat, the Major came across the walk so he could pass me where I would have to salute him. I walked to the PX to say goodbye to one of the soldiers. Here comes the Major again. I did not salute him.

"Soldier, I am going to put you on report for not giving the proper salute."

I said, "Sir, did you leave the compound?"

"You know damn well, I didn't."

"Well, sir, if you left then you would have gotten another salute. Since you didn't, you were only entitled to one salute and you know the regulations."

He didn't know what to say. Then he sputtered, "Have that jacket cleaned."

"It was cleaned an hour ago with all my other clothes. I am well aware of army regulations, something you should check up on. Good-bye."

"Where do you think you are going?" Just then the truck driver called out, "You civilians want a ride to the train to go home or do you want to join up again?"

I said, "Not with this asshole like this major. One day in combat this jackass would shit his pants." We were off to the train. The Sergeant added, "You don't know how good it is that some one told him off. Even the officers don't like him."

How he became a Major was beyond me. We were civilians and he wasn't aware of it.

In August of 1945, back in the States, my first leave in over two years, many of us had gone overseas right after basic training and never had a chance to go home. I was on a 30-day leave. I stopped over to visit my sister-in-law, my older brother's wife. She was working in the local canning factory. I couldn't believe my eyes --- German prisoners of war working side-by-side with our American women and in Europe our service men are behind barbed wire fences with harsh treatment. While I was on leave, the Japanese surrendered. The whole town was celebrating. I was in a nearby tavern when an old friend slapped me on the back to welcome me home and the war was over. My sister-in-law told me that I turned and flattened him out. I didn't recall doing it. So the next day I looked him up and told him how sorry I was, and that it might happen again. It was a hard lesson. And he said 'let's go have a beer'. When I left to go back to camp, this fellow drove me to the train and hugged me.

Chapter Four
Raising a Family

My day of discharge came on January 9, 1946. Once on the train homeward bound for good, I found a seat, hung my jacket so the medal wouldn't rub against the wall and hung my cane. The train filled with a mix of servicemen. In came this most beautiful American girl. She looked at my jacket and cane and asked if she could sit with me. What else could I say except 'yes'? Wow, did the men whoop it up. No sooner than she sat down, she opened a small suitcase and out came the book of "Forever Amber".

"Did you read this book?" she asked.

"No, but I was told about the contents." I noticed she had an empty whiskey bottle in her suitcase. I said to myself, why would she carry an empty? We did some small talk then she showed me a diamond ring. It was no dime store ring. She said it was a four-carat diamond. She was talking about the ring and the Captain that gave it to her. She didn't say if he died, maybe she dumped him. I didn't believe that he died. There was no remorse. She said her home was in Detroit and she gave me her address. She was clever and when we were not talking, she was asleep on my chest. I told myself, Tony, watch out. You are no match for this lady. She's been around.

When we were getting close to Buffalo, she wanted to know if there was any hotel close by. We could stay for the day and she could catch the later train. I said that I was not from this part of the city. There was a lay over for the train so we got off and went to the train restaurant and had breakfast. I walked her back to the train. I watched which servicemen she would pick. She picked another serviceman with a cane. She knew all the men who were discharged --- had a few hundred dollars on them --- and she would find a sucker. She knew all about later train departures; maybe this was her game to make money.

When I got to the areas where families were waiting, I was surprised that my stepfather was there, and he carried my Army duffel bag. Home at last, after almost three years. After a few days, I wanted to visit all of the people who had written to me. My first visit was the mother of Tom, the guy I had met at the train when we went into the service. I got out before Tom and told her who I was and that Tom was all right and being discharged. I visited her everyday until Tom came home. She lived only a block from our house.

I visited all the ladies from St. Patrick church just to thank them for the church newspaper. I visited all the beautiful ladies who wrote to me. There was one more lady I had to visit. I worked with her husband and son in Bell Aircraft but I had never met this lady; she was my first fan mail. In basic training and throughout the war, she sent package after package. I knew she was a very sick lady. Her husband used to tell me of her heart problems when we worked together. She was bed ridden for many, many years. Then, when I went overseas, I told her she could stop writing because if anything happened to me I didn't want her to feel bad; she kept writing. Little did I know she would become my future sister-in-law.

I visited this lady many times. One day asked me if I would go to the drug store for her and she gave me a note. I came back with a box of Kotex. On one of my visits her son and his wife came over while we were all having dinner.

The son said, "My aunt and uncle are going to Crystal Beach, would you like to come?"

I said, "Yes, I'd never been to that beach."

Joe Jr. said, "My Aunt Ida should have been here with you."

His Aunt Vera said, "Dad, wouldn't like that."

"Where is your Aunt Ida?" I asked.

"I can't tell you that. Gramps would get a shotgun after me."

I said, "I faced the whole German army. One man with a shotgun wouldn't scare me." All this time this sick lady was telling her sister, Ida, about me.

In the early part of my story, I mentioned about a little girl that we would meet again when I was ten and she was eight. Who would have thought she would be come my wife. She is the sister of the sick lady who wrote to me. I worked with her husband in Bell Aircraft.

The very next day I visited Phyl, the sick lady. I asked her what her maiden name was and asked where her father lived. She gave me the address. The next day I wrote Ida a letter. I told her who I was and that I had been writing to her sister for over two years. She wrote: 'I know who you are.'

I got a reply so fast that the letters could have passed in transit. Joe Sr., the sick lady's husband, gave me a ride to Ida's house. He said Ida's mother and father were old-fashioned; they thought they still lived in Italy. He also said there might be a problem.

I told him, "Just tell them I was in Italy and I can bring them up-to-date about Italy, and I can answer any questions they have."

My brother-in-law to be was quite nervous. He figured he was going to get feedback why I was there. We went to the front room. Ida sat in one corner of the room and me in the other on the same wall. This way we couldn't look at each other, yet there was a connection; we both felt it. Of all the beautiful ladies I met, there never was a connection. That changed when I met Ida.

I didn't have a car. I had to catch a bus and travel thirty miles to see her and wait all day at her other sister's house a block away. The parents made sure that Ida was not at home. She was the last one old enough to bring home the money. The other two were too young. The parents figured if she was not home I would leave and go back home. If she wasn't available on weekends I would stop coming. This went on for seven months until I got my mother in the picture and lay down the law about how things are done in America. And she told Ida's mother to speak up and defend your daughter.

I'd taken Ida out three times before we got married.

The father wanted to go to an Italian stage show in Buffalo. Who do you think paid for the tickets? They were going to sit Ida between them but I grabbed Ida and said 'you sit next to me. I understood one word in Italian and it meant codfish. We went two more times in local shows. I'd push Ida ahead and pay for two --- her sister Sara and her husband had to be with us otherwise Ida couldn't go.

On Ida's birthday we got engaged and the father wanted to set our wedding day, that was the day that Ida would start her period. That's when my mother really got into the act and lay into the father and mother in Italian so they had no problems understanding her. Mother spoke to Ida and the date was set for Oct. 5th, 1946.

On one of my visits to Ida's home, I was taking the Greyhound bus home, Ida's young sister gave me a piece of gum. I thought it was one of the Chiclets gums. Well, it was not. I told the bus driver that 'when you get to a big tree, stop. I have to go and it's not my water.' We stopped and waited for me to get back and there was a lot of laughter. I was told later that piece of gum was a freemint--- also known to be as efficient as Ex-lax.

When I got out of the service, my sister Frances was taking up typing so I bought her a typewriter. I must explain that when my parents had a second daughter, she was also named Frances after the first Frances that died.

My younger brother, Lewis, was interested in boxing. Every time when there was a local fight, he would go and see it. So when I got out of the service I bought him boxing gloves and boxed with him. There were rules: no punching in the face, and I told him before he became a boxer that he would have to beat me first. He was damn good. After a few boxing bouts, I believe he figured he could take me. He gave me a fast one to the lip. I, in return, gave him a fast one to the stomach. He bent over and went to the porch and leaned over the railing. I figured he was going to puke. I believe we boxed one more time without rules and after a couple of punches, he got dizzy. And that was the end of his boxing career. He could hold his own in any fight; he was good. My whole family was pretty close then. My youngest brother, Bobby, always put a note in my Mother's letters to me. I didn't have any pictures of my sister Frances. I had a picture of my youngest sister, Julia, and carried it throughout the war.

When Ida had a wedding shower, I didn't have a car as yet, still travelling by bus but I had rented a house three months before we got married. When the shower was over I was given three shopping bags of shower gifts to take to our house. It was raining so my future father-in-law gave me his raincoat to wear. When I got off the bus and starting walking, a car pulled up and two men got out and pushed me against Clark Oasis wall. They wanted to know what was in the bags.

"Who the hell are you?" I demanded.

"We're cops," he said, and showed me his badge.

"Why didn't you just say so instead of pushing me against the wall."

The other officer said, "We are looking for a thief. You fit the picture with that long raincoat.

"They're shower gifts and the raincoat belongs to my father-in-law to be. I am going to our house, three blocks down, next to the tavern, that I am renting."

They let me go and followed me all the way. You would think that they would give me a ride due to the rain. They waited until

I left my flat and watched me walk another five blocks to my Mother's house.

It was the custom of the older Italian families to celebrate St. Joseph's Day by having an open table of food and everyone was welcome. On this St. Joseph's Day, March 1946, my in-laws to be had a table altar and all. One of the candles started a fire; everyone ran out. I ran into the room and started pulling down the curtains and everything that was burning. I called for someone to get the sick lady out of the bed. I was the only one fighting the fire. My hair on my arms sizzled and burned then Ida came in and put a towel on my face and arms to quench the heat. After the fire was put out, I did all the repairs on the house and paid all of my doctor's bills. I even got them a good settlement for the insurance company. I stayed there while I was repairing the house, then one married sister said to her mother that it didn't look good for me staying there when Ida and me were not yet married. So after all the repairs, I was told to just come on weekends.

While visiting my girl, my wife to be, she was picking strawberries on their property. Her little brother had a BB gun shooting at tin cans. I tested the gun to see what range and impact it had. Ida was about two hundred feet away and was bending over to pick up her tray of berries. The temptation was too great so I aimed and fired a shot. She jumped and grabbed her leg. Her father thought a bee stung her. When she saw me with the BB gun, she came after me with a handful of strawberries. Her father got a big kick out of it when she tried to rub my face with her berries.

Ida wanted to get the furniture before we got married. Her mother wanted to go with her. My mother stepped into the picture again. She said that it will be their furniture and they will pick it out. You and I will do some shopping. We were almost set. We had a flat and furniture, now we needed Ida's wedding gown. We picked out the wedding gown the same day. I paid for everything, including the wedding gown. We were all set; all we had to do was get married.

We got married on October 5th in Silver Creek, New York in Mt. Carmel church, officiated by Monsieur O'Conner. The bride took my breath away. She was the most beautiful woman I ever saw. There was only one bottle of whiskey and it broke the oldest brother in-law. He said it was for me; I shared it with him. About noon we left and went to my Mother's house to catch a train but to our surprise my stepfather and Mother had another party for us. My stepfather had some of his friends and kin there.

Soon after, we left for New York City on our honeymoon and stayed at Hotel Woodstock. I waited a long time before my new wife came to bed. Her sister scared her by telling her what was going to happen on her first night. I tried to be patient.

In the morning, I went down to the lobby to buy some cards and brought them back to the room. We began writing our thank-you cards when someone knocked on the door, and knocked again. It was a woman's voice calling for Ida. I looked at my wife and said if that's your mother not letting you alone on your honeymoon, I am going to throw her out of the window. Enough is enough! I was pissed. I opened the door and said, "What in the hell do you want?" Then I saw a black lady.

"I want to see Ida."

"Why do you want to talk to my wife?"

"I don't want to talk to your wife. I want to talk to the maid named Ida."

"There's no one here," I said, rather irritated.

Then my wife spoke up. "While you were in the lobby, a maid came. She is in the bathroom." The maid came out of the bathroom. "I told them the whole story of my courtship," she said. I had to admit Ida was grateful to confide in someone.

They laughed so hard I thought they were going to wet themselves. I said I was sorry, the way I spoke to her. She understood.

We were off to the Statue of Liberty. It was some climb to the top. We didn't know there was an elevator that went part way. There was a lady in front of us that was so fat and this French stairway was so narrow that she grabbed one side of her body to pull it through then the other side. She never made it to the top. She was told to stop in a small rest area until the rest of the group went up. She had to go back down.

We toured New York for a few days. We went to see Paul Whiteman's show and left to Orange City, New Jersey to see Ida's aunt and uncle. This was also funny, but not at the time. There were two big rooms with a big open arch and a bed in each room. The uncle slept in one room. He didn't get any sleep that night. We went to bed first. I told Ida that these old type springs make a lot of noise and your uncle is going to sleep in that bed. I was right; he sat up all night watching us. I slept at the edge of the bed and Ida on the other side. This must have puzzled him --- just married and not together.

In the morning, we left and went to see my aunt in Raritan, New Jersey. I told my aunt what happened. She said, "You gotta close the door." That was funny.

From there we went to our little flat. I paid sixteen dollars a month and two dollars under the table toward a rent ceiling. When we got to our flat, Mother had food in our house for a whole week and had the bride and groom figurines from the cake in the middle of the table all set up. Never in my lifetime have I seen a mother in-law and a daughter in-law get along so well. They were like two peas in a pod until the day Mother died at the age of ninety-nine.

On our first Christmas of 1946, I was very sick and not able to work, and had only twenty-six cents between us. I was not working due to a service-related stomach problem. I was sent to Batavia, New York Veterans Hospital. There was a big fat Major sitting at the desk and a line of veterans to pass by him. He would tell each veteran that their problem was in their head. A veteran with shrapnel in his shoulder, who was standing in front of me, was told that the shrapnel in his shoulder was no problem and there was no pain. The pain was in his head. And then it was my turn with stomach pain. I told the Major, "If you say it's in my head, what are you going to say if I punch you in the mouth? Is it in your head that you got hurt?"

They decided to give me thirty-percent for nervous condition. As a veteran I went in training under Public Law 16. My first training was at Bond's Clothing factory pressing flies on men's pants. From there I learned how to do dry cleaning, and after that a fish market store. No matter how much you washed, when you got on a bus everyone turned to look at you. At home, it was just as bad. One day at the fish store, I had to go in the deep freeze and get this very large fish. It had frozen with a big bend in it. I put it on the table to work on it a little later. I moved the fish closer to me. The bend or curve or whatever you want to call it, the heat made it unbend and it suddenly hit me on the nose. I fell backward about a foot. That was the last straw. Between the smell and a dead fish nailing me, I quit.

After I finished these three work courses, I got a check from the VA for, I believe, $992 dollars. I went back to the VA and told them that they had made a mistake. For two hours we went over the books, and they said I was wrong and the check was mine. I said, let me look again and I saw that on each project I got sort of a bonus. I found the error and now I was told that I owed the VA $400 dollars. I should have put it in the bank and collected the interest; they never would have found it. As much as I needed money, I knew it wasn't mine. And I never got any thank-you letter.

My father in-law wanted his letter read and asked me to bring him to this Italian car dealer to read it. The car dealer wanted me to be a driver. I told him that I wasn't that good of a driver to move new cars around. He said he wanted me as his personal driver. I thanked him and said no. About two weeks later, a bunch of Mafia leaders got arrested and he was one of them. I am sure glad I didn't take that job. When I told my father in-law, he was shocked. That arrest caused me to lose a job at an all-girls school. I was told to start on a Monday but Friday headlines had the Mafia story. They told me they hired the old man back. Being Italian I knew better; I said nothing and left.

October 5th of 1947, started out as a good day. It was our one-year of marriage and time to celebrate. My stepfather and I had a few drinks at my home. I said to my wife and mother that we had to go over to pick up my godmother and her husband two blocks away and have them come to our party. It was only one block away. Before I left, I gave my wife my wallet to hold. My wife called their home about twenty minutes later and asked for me. They said I hadn't arrived so my wife and mother and stepfather came to look for me --- and they found me laying flat on the ground. I was dazed and said a black man wanted to rob me, hit me on the head with a pipe, and knocked me out. Once at my god mother's daughter's house, I went to the sink and my stepfather grabbed me because I was starting to fall. I thought he was the black man. I grabbed the sink so hard, I pulled it off the wall. My stepfather, only five foot nine and about 185 pounds, and my godmother's son in-law, only five eight and 200 pounds couldn't break me away from the sink. So my stepfather cut off my air. When my head cleared up from being knocked out, I said I was sorry and fixed the sink the next day.

One winter we went to the bottom of Niagara Falls. The water that wasn't running was frozen and looked like a mountain of ice. It looked beautiful. A gust of wind shot up and blew a whole wall of ice water on us and almost blew us right off the area we were standing on. It was a real close call. We were frozen. We rushed to the car and put the heater on and drove home about thirty miles. That was the last trip to the bottom of the falls.

As my wife and I were walking down Main Street on our way to see a movie, I had my new black suit on, as people were walking past us they started to laugh. This went on for awhile and I asked my wife what are they laughing about? Is my fly open? I went to get the tickets. The ticket man said, "Sir, you have pigeon goo on the left side of your jacket."

Now I was not going back home because this was a special day for us. I asked where the men's room was. I removed my jacket and noticed some on my pants. I washed the jacket and then removed my pants and washed it off. I went back to the ticket booth and got our tickets. I don't recall the movie but afterward we went for a banana split and went home. The end of a beautiful day.

When first trained, one of the jobs I had was selling women's dresses and corsets. This job didn't set too well with my wife since I had to measure the women for corsets. I tried my hand as a demonstrator in Grant's Department Store selling plastic wipe-on polish for furniture. I was doing okay until they wanted me to travel to different towns, so I quit.

After we got married, things were better between my stepfather and me. He treated my wife well and when the first born was able to walk, he would take him for a stroll. Our son was taught to call him Grampa as soon as he was able to talk. About three days before Ted died, we were at their home all sitting around the table. He said, "Anthony, if I had to do everything all over again, I would have treated you better. You are the best of the sons even when we never got along. You taught them to call me Grampa."

I thanked him and said all is fine. I believe he knew he had a very bad heart but never said anything to Ma. It takes quite a man to say he was wrong and I respected him for that. Once in awhile I dream about him and now Mother is with him. I do believe we left as friends. He did leave me with a wonderful sister, his daughter, Julia.

While working at Westinghouse as a grinder, I was charged with grinding the inside of electric motor casings to a mirror finish. I used a big air hand-grinder, wore my glasses and safety goggles and a plastic shield. One time the 150 pound air pressure hose broke and it blew all the fine metal off my apron, under my shield and safety goggles and right into my eyes. The doctor told me that I had some old scars dead center of my pupils. I believe it was the dirt of a shell explosive that I washed out and was issued glasses in the hospital while I was overseas.

I put in a bid to the electrical department, working on the big battery trucks. My job was to get them charged and to take care of three big 240 generators. This one truck had a round front. To push items in place you had to sit on the seat for it to make a forward or backward movement. Standing on the floor in front of this truck, I flipped the seat back and the truck suddenly moved forward and pinned me against another truck. This should not have happened. What saved my life was the electrician's belt with all my tools and the flashlight. The flashlight and batteries were flat. I pushed the 6000-pound truck back so I could get out. I then got on a gasoline industrial truck and went to the nurse and told her what happened. She said she was alone and that I would have to put the heating pad on myself. "Your problem is below the belt," she told me. "When you're finished you can leave."

I told her, "I need help to get up on the table. What are you afraid of? I am in a lot of pain. I am not interested in you." Twenty minutes later I went back to my station, hooked up the rest of the trucks, punched out and walked about a fourth of a mile to my car, then drove ten miles home. I was now feeling the pain and limping. My wife knew something was wrong as soon as I got in the door. I went directly to bed. I got up the next morning and stepped on the floor and fell. I could not stand. Ida called the plant doctor and was told if I was feeling that bad that we should call our doctor. Doctors made house calls back then. Our doctor said that I had a fractured pelvis; they rushed me to the hospital. I found out that my bladder was all scarred up and it was a miracle that it didn't rupture.

After three months, I tried to return to work. I was told if I can't do the work, go home. The job required me to pull 1200-pound batteries into position to be charged, climb a ten-foot ladder, and start the generators. I told them I lived in Angola and I came with a driver. They said then wait until he gets out of work. But that was eight hours later. I left and decided to hitchhike home. I got to the highway then a fellow worker was driving by and stopped to ask me what was going on. I explained that they wouldn't give me a ride home and he said get in the car and I will take you home. The distance was 45 miles away and he lived locally in Buffalo. This fellow worker went out of his way and made a 90 mile round trip. I was home for the next nine and a half years because they wouldn't give me light duty and no one else would hire me while I was receiving workers' compensation. When I was in the hospital the company's Safety Officer asked me if I had let the truck hit me on purpose.

Whether it was from the accident or not, that same year I had a gall bladder operation. My wife never complained. She was always there. Trying to be active, I learned how to wallpaper.

I was wallpapering our house. It had a protruding chimney that did not protrude from a flat wall. It was part of the arch to the next room. My wife did the entire pasting and handed me the wallpaper. I had one panel up and asked he if it was straight; her reply was 'it was perfect', so the next two panels went up and I asked the same question, and again she said 'perfect'. I could see something was wrong. I got down and checked for myself; I could see a slant. I got back on the ladder and ripped all the panels off the wall, and said, "Just paste, and don't say anything." It ended up a perfect job. You could not see where the seams met.

One night I wanted a cigar, so I got on my bicycle; it was a dark night. I hit a pothole and was told later that that I flew over the handlebars and fell on my face. I don't know how I got home. The next thing I knew, a doctor was putting the final stitches on my face. My wife said that two boys on the street saw it happen and got me home with my bicycle. Until this day I don't remember two and a half hours of my life. I saw a lawyer and he and the city gave me five hundred dollars, and we were able to buy a TV.

My friend, Tom, that I had meet at the train station when we went into the service, said to me, "Tony, you need a car. I will teach you and you use my car for the test." He was a great guy. He was there for my wedding and for all of the pictures that he had taken, he gave us copies. Thanks to Tom we have pictures.

Tom needed another man for a ball game and got me to play. We won and I got a dollar. The loser had to pay the winning team. We stayed in touch every Christmas for fifty-five years until he passed away. We did see Tom two years before he passed away.

What a great feeling. Thanks to Tom, got my driver's license. I bought a 1935 Chevrolet and now was able to go into the house painting business. And by word-of-mouth I had many houses to paint. I was hired to paint Detective Kirby's house. It was a two-story. I had to tie a section of my 36-foot ladder to my 40-foot ladder in order to reach the peak of his house over the front porch. Some kid came along with his dog and the dog went under the ladder. The dog's rope pulled the ladder and the paint spilled all over the porch roof. I used thinner to try to clean it up. I wonder to this day if the thinner ruined the shingles. Detective Kirby never said a word. In fact, he got me another gallon of paint. He liked my painting and got me another job – and was glad I wasn't hurt.

Most homes in Buffalo were two-story. I figured it would take a week to paint a home. I would charge $200 dollars per home and the homeowner would furnish the paint. If I furnished the paint, it would cost $300 dollars plus the cost of the paint. I got a contract to paint this three-story building with a steeple.

It was in bad shape. I got my younger brother, Lewis, to help me on that job.

Lewis and I tied the eighteen-foot section of the ladder to the forty-foot ladder. I went to the third floor and dropped one end of the rope so it could secure the ladder. I then pulled the ladder up while my brother held the ladder in place. We now had to put four sixteen-penny nails in each of three two-by-ten planks so they would go over the ladder rungs. This was to secure the ladder so it wouldn't slide. I carried the planks to each floor and handed them to my brother and placed the nails over the rungs. Once secure, I would nail my end to the windowsill to make it sturdy. We could not reach the steeple windows to paint. We entered the steeple room from the flat roof and opened the steeple door.

We then had another problem; those windows were about thirteen inches wide. After taking out the lower window and checking to see how sturdy the upper windows were, we then put the two-by-ten plank in the window and let it hang out about two feet. I nailed one end to the floor and the other to the sill.

I climbed up on the board, grabbed the bottom of the upper window, and got in a standing position and began painting the window frame. I was precariously standing two feet out of the window on a ten-inch plank. There was a lot of traffic going by and people gathering around. The police moved them on. I was glad that was over.

We now had the flagpole perched on top of the steeple. It was an old pole, gray with deep cracks. My brother got on the roof and got a rope around it. I told him to paint from the roof side. In case the pole broke, he could slide to the roof, not to the street some sixty feet below. The pole was firm and got its coat of paint. Some fifty years later, it has the same paint job.

When jobs got slow, I helped my old landlord who was the janitor at St. Patrick's church for thirty-eight cents per hour, and fixed old houses he bought and got fifty cents per hour --- all extra side money.

There was an attic that I remodeled into a full-finished bedroom. One night, as we were laying down to go to sleep, a storm was howling and lightning came through the window about a foot above our heads. It hit the corner of the chimney and went out the window on the other side of the attic.

On this property, the lean-to part of the shed was about twenty feet from the railroad tracks. The first night in this house when we went to sleep the train blew its whistle and the roar of the train made us jump out of bed. We thought the train was coming through the house. After the remodeling was finished, he put it up for sale.

After my plant accident, I was sent to all kinds of special doctors and admitted to hospitals for spinal taps, nerve blocks --- you name it, I got it. I was receiving $31 dollars weekly compensation checks and they would stop my checks. One time they stopped the checks for eighteen months. My wife had to go to work at an onion factory peeling onions. On one of my trips to the doctor for treatments, I got stuck about ten miles from Buffalo. It was one of the worst snowstorms in years. It got so bad that snowplows were not able to move. I was lucky that I had a full tank of gas. I was stranded in my car from ten a.m. until noon the next day. There were no buildings in this area and if there was one, you won't have been able to get to it. I had no way of letting my wife know that I was sitting in my car all night, struggling to keep warm yet opening the window a little when I used the heater to get rid of the fumes. When the snowplows got through, I drove to the doctor's office and called my wife. She was worried sick.

When I was working, I made five thousand dollars a year, and after nine and a half years my case was settled for eleven thousand. The lawyer got a thousand; he could have gotten more. At five thousand a year plus raises if I was working, I lost a bundle of money.

No one offered to help us for all of those years except my mother and my nephew, Joe, the son of the sick lady. Our refrigerator went out and Joe came up with one. What a great guy. He is no longer with us. There was one relative who came up when he heard I got a settlement and wanted me to loan him two thousand dollars. I said, "And where were you for the past nine and a half years?"

After my settlement, I applied to the Veterans Hospital for a job. They gave me a hard time. After weeks of waiting, I went to the hospital to check up on my application at the personnel clerk. He said that he didn't send it through.

I asked, "Why not?"

"You have a nervous condition from the war."

I said, "So you are now a doctor? You decide if a person has a nervous problem then he must be a psycho because he is nervous?"

He said, "Calm down. You can catch more flies with honey than with vinegar."

"You can stick the honey paper on your nose after I go to the newspaper and state that you decide a veteran is a psycho because he is nervous." He started to shake. 'Why are you shaking? Are you a psycho?"

I got the job as a cook's helper but I got my first case of pneumonia going from a twenty-degree freezer to a hundred-degree kitchen. After going to the hospital's doctor for this cold, he wanted me to take a few days off. The woman director said 'no'; she over ruled the doctor. I went back to the doctor. He told me to 'go home on your own --- you have pneumonia.'

This was my third month of work. My wife told me to quit and I did.

When I moved back to the city. We were renting free. The owner's young son was a problem with is father. The son would swear at him and tell him off. He said, "I am divorced. Your son is the same age as my son, can you help him?"

I said that I would and I won't lay a hand on him. When I left, this ten-year-old made a one hundred and eighty degree turn. The neighbors couldn't believe it. His father's wife wanted to move back in with the new husband. The father had no backbone. I had to move. I was told about a house for sale and I wanted to rent it in the meantime. I went to this lady and told her my situation. She wanted to know how long before I would get a settlement, and I said maybe one or two years. She said that was all right, and charged us sixty dollars per month, and when I receive my settlement, all the money I paid for rent would become my down payment. All she wanted us to do was to pay the taxes for that year. This was our first big break, thanks to a kind lady.

When it was time to purchase the house, I called the kind lady and told her my case was settled, and that I was going to put in for a loan to buy the house. I asked her if the deal was still on and she said that it was. On my loan statement, I said I was in the TV repair business and had a business license. I was hoping they didn't know anything about TVs. I had six TVs turned so that all the wiring could be seen, some mirrors and electronic equipment that i had built was placed in view. I was never asked what my yearly income was but the loan went through and the house was ours.

I was happy but also going under a lot of stress not working for nine and a half years, and sweating out the bank plus my post-traumatic stress from the war, that, and my wife had to go to work upset me. I forgot I had taken my daily pill and mistakenly took another that caused me to fall backward. My son said I hit my head on the metal grate. The next thing I saw was my wife standing there with her foreman from America Machine foundry. I said: "What's going on?" She said that our son had called her at work and that I had fallen and had not moved. The foreman told my wife to stay home with me and he left.

I got a job at a nursing home as a janitor. For lunch the tables were separated: nurses and supervisors at one table, all others at another table. As a new worker, no one introduced themselves to me. They all thought I was Spanish or a foreigner, and that I could not speak English. All but one would say 'maybe he is from Mexico', 'maybe a 'wetback' or from Italy', 'maybe Mafia'. This went on for four days. This one guy got a kick out of Mafia talk. I never let on that I understood everything. The other table was listening to everything that was said, and said nothing. I spoke to one of the nurses and asked her not to say anything, and tell the other nurses not to let on because I was going to surprise them when the right time came.

This one woman didn't go along with all this talking and told them from day one 'he's American and understands and speaks English.' This Mafia talking dude said, "If he is American why doesn't he speak?" This lady winked at me a couple of times and I would nod my head when no one was looking.

This one day, the dude was going full blast about the Mafia. I got up, walked near the other table, and winked. They all stopped eating. As I went behind the Mafia talking dude, I grabbed him by the shoulder and growled, "Pass me the butter or you will die ---Mafia style."

He turned as white as a ghost and almost fell out of the chair.

"All of you people should have listened to that lady when she said I was American and understood English. Instead of welcoming a new worker, you were downgrading him. If by chance I have connections with the Mafia, I am not saying one way or the other, you could be in a lot of trouble with a pair of cement shoes." And with that, I smiled and left the room.

One night I had my nephew come by and ask for me. My nephew was a big, rough-looking gut with a rough voice. The clerk, who happened to be the Mafia talking dude, stared at my nephew. He told the clerk, "I'm looking for Mister Pasqualetti and be quick about it."

This scared the hell out of him. I found out where the dude lived and put a Black Hand on his door. A couple of days later he came to me. He thought someone was following him and he ducked into one of the deep cellar windows that set below the pavement. As weeks went by, we became good friends and I asked him if he found a Black Hand on his door. I told him that I put it there to teach him a lesson about loose talk, and that he was lucky I was not Mafia. Years after I left, we were still good friends.

While I was getting $31 dollars a week for compensation, my wife and our two children had taken two young children – one girl and a three-year-old boy. The father working long hours was causing a problem. They were separated. The father could not work and take care of the children. Being good friends of the couple, we had taken the children in so they could come to terms. We had the children for three months.

The mother told us that their other young daughter was to have her Holy Communion, and she didn't have a dress for the occasion, so we loaned her our daughter's Holy Communion dress. We got a nice suit from the church for the little boy.

He started out cleaning pools. They were new to California where he then established his own swimming pool business selling chemicals to other pool men. The couple patched things up and had a happy marriage for over fifty years until he passed away.

While my checks were stopped for eighteen months, I sold my big table saw with a 110 and 220-watt motor with all the cutters and dado blades. The saw and all the attachments were worth $400 dollars. I was behind two months rent. The landlord said he would take my saw and all the attachments for the two-month's rent. Our rent was only $45 dollars a month; a $400 dollar saw for $90 dollars in rent --- I had no choice. Talking about hitting a person when he is down; this was it. For the third and fourth month, the welfare paid the rent but I had to sign a paper to pay it back. On the fifth month, my wife got a job.

We lived upstairs and the landlord lived downstairs on this 150-acre farm. We had a female Doxie whose name was Sandy. The first night she killed thirteen rats in the upstairs outside hallway within one hour. Sandy was a great hunter. While I was hunting a woodchuck, Sandy saw it and I said 'get it'. And I was standing there waiting for Sandy to flush it out, when here she came with it in her mouth; I didn't need a gun.

One night about 2 a.m., Sandy came into our bedroom barking her head off and wouldn't leave. I smelled smoke. The oil stove was in the front room. If it caught on fire the door would be blocked and we would all have to jump out the second floor window. I got the landlord and we carried the stove outside. Sandy saved our lives and the house.

Sandy came into our bedroom one more time barking her head off again. This time the phone was ringing. I got to the phone and heard my name and the phone went dead. It was the landlord that I had worked with at the church. It was twenty degrees outside and I could not start my car so I woke up my landlord. We got into his car and drove to the house. It was locked up tighter than a drum. The shed part of the door had a crossed board to secure it. We pulled the car up next to the window and broke it so I could get in. Once inside, I let my landlord in and the inside door was locked, too. The landlord kicked that door in. With the door open we thought the house was on fire so much heat hit us. It had to be over 110 degrees. All the windows were locked. Mike was passed out by the phone. His wife was also on the floor. We opened all the windows and the landlord called the ambulance. Sandy saved another family.

I went to the hospital to check on them and then home to get my other dog and bring it to Mike's house. I tied the dog in the kitchen, not far from the broken door. While I was getting clothes for Mike and his wife, I heard Peppe, our boxer-pit bull mix, barking. He already had a man cornered who was going to rob the house. Another good deed for the dog. Mike and his wife were okay, and I helped move them back to the city.

On this farm, the landlord got Jamaican workers to come up every summer to work the 150 acres of grapes. They were to stay at his brother's farm about a half mile away. But they were known to come to our area around the house when there was no work. There were only two women who lived there: my wife and the landlord's wife and a lot of chickens. The landlord told me to get rid of any trespassers if they come up after he went to work. So this one morning, I went out and said, "What are you doing up here? There's no work for you, and this is not a hang out. I will shoot anybody that doesn't belong here."

There was a small bird on the top rack of the truck about 30 feet away. I raised my .25 automatic and fired. I shot the bird's head off. I never saw them up around our place again unless there was work, and away from the house. Then they told the landlord how I shot a bird's head off at a good distance. He said, "That's nothing. If he uses his .357, he will knock your eyes out at a hundred feet. He is a crack shot." And he wasn't lying when he said that.

When my dogs needed treatment, I got free medical for them. When he had a few surgeries to do, I would help him. On one operation, the dog let out a blast of hot air and blood hit me in the face. He laughed. He always chewed tobacco and grabbed a mouthful while he had blood and hair on his hands. Once I had to rush sandy to him because she ate rat poison. He said, "Did she have anything to eat before the poison?"

"Yes," I said, "Four hot dogs, his food, and a plate of spaghetti."

Sandy got a shot. He said that she ate so much that the poison didn't have time to react, and the shot would take care of the poison.

One day we came home from shopping. I put seven steaks on the table and my wife called me to hang a mirror in the bathroom. When I got back there were only six steaks left. Sandy was under the chair and the steak was gone in less than two minutes. She was a fine dog. I always had Sandy along when I coached the kids' ball games.

One time, I was rushed to the Columbus Hospital for an appendix operation. While waiting to go to the operating room, a little boy came up to my bedside and said, "Don't be afraid. I will be in this bed next to you when you come back."

When I did return he got out of the bed and came to me and said, "I told you it would be all right." It was now the little boy's turn for an operation.

"I will be there for you, so don't worry. You see," I told him, "I came out all right."

In the morning, the nurse came looking for me. They didn't bring the little boy back to my room. They had moved him to the second floor. I was at his side and he said with a big smile.

"They changed my room and I got scared. I thought something went wrong."

"Nothing is wrong. This is the children's ward and I will come to see you again before I leave."

Just then the nurse came up and scolded me. "You just had an operation. You should be in bed." The nurse told the doctor that I went to the second floor to see a little boy. The doctor said, "He's all right. In combat, they are back on the line in three to four days."

My wife's experience in the hospital was for our newest baby. My wife went through fifty-four hours of straight labor. She was in lots of pain. Her doctor had to leave the hospital for an emergency and told the head doctor to check my wife every fifteen minutes. Twenty minutes went by, then thirty, and no doctor. Forty minutes had come and gone so I asked the nurse, "Where is this doctor? He is supposed to check my wife every fifteen minutes, and she's in a lot of pain."

"He's in a meeting," she said.

I opened the meeting room door and there he was drinking coffee.

"You were supposed to check my wife every fifteen minutes and an hour has gone by, and you never got off your fat ass. Get your fat ass out there and check her. And I hope you drop dead."

After he checked my wife, he stepped out of the room and fell to the floor. They all thought I gave him a heart attack. The head nurse said something to me and I told her to shut her mouth or she would be next. Just then our assigned doctor came in and wanted to know what happened. He checked the doctor out and said that he had no heart attack. The doctor said that I had shook him up and it was about time someone put him in his place. My wife gave me our first born on January 16th, 1948. A son named Anthony, Jr. Our new neighbor was a great help and Mother was also a great help.

I decided I needed a better car and decided to sell my old 1935 Chevrolet but it needed a paint job. There was a paint glove out to paint cars. The paint job looked great so I sold it to a black man that I knew who worked in the canning factory in Irving, the town where my wife use to live. The next year when he came back from the south to find work again, he said, "Tony, what kind of paint job did you get on that car?"

"Why do you ask?" I said.

"When it rained, it all came off but it's a good running car."

I didn't tell him that I didn't know you had to sand the car so the paint would stick. I felt bad; he was a very nice guy.

I bought a 1939 Plymouth and on weekends I would go to an Italian bakery and buy day old bread, then head on to the Irving Canning factory in Irving, New York to sell the bread to the Italian families that worked there.

While working at Westinghouse our second child was born. A girl named Patricia Ann. I got a call that my wife was rushed to the hospital. I got into my high speed rear-end Plymouth and drove ten miles to the hospital and got there before the taxicab, and he had to drive only two miles. I had to wait until he got there and then I gave him hell. My wife had no problem with this birth. In fact, this baby didn't wait. She wanted to be born now. Mother and child were doing fine on May 7th, 1952.

One night Ida and I went fishing in Irving, New York. That night I decided to fish next to the Irving steel bridge. The creek that ran under the bridge separated US lands from Indian lands. It was very good fishing there. I had my Coleman lantern and raincoat just in case it rained. My wife stayed in the car close enough so we could talk. Sitting there for about an hour and no fish. It started to rain. They say it's good fishing when it rains and right after the rain, it started to thunder. My wife said for me to quit but I said I was all right; I had my raincoat. It was just a light rain but ten minutes later it started to pour, and the lightning smacked. My wife was getting real nervous. Just about this time, I hooked something big and had a hard time reeling it in – and my wife yelling for me to quit.

I said, "I have a channel cat."

"I don't care. Quit!"

The lightning hit the bridge on the far side across the creek. I walked next to the cement wall down the bank struggling with my pole. This was something big. The storm was getting bad, so I let my line scrape along the cement so it would break. I got my equipment and went home, disappointed but safe.

On the weekend we went back to Irving to visit with my in-laws, I was talking to a black man named Frank, a good friend and fishing partner. He said to me that where I was fishing a few nights ago -- and I said, "yes, I lost a big fish."—He said, "Yes, I know. I caught your twenty-two pound channel cat, your weights and hooks were still on the fish when I caught it. I knew it was your weights."

"I'm glad it was you that caught it," I told him. The storm was real bad otherwise I would have stayed and tried to land it. I believe the year was 1947, the year the "big one" got away.

When Anthony, our son, was about four years old, I had him fishing with Frank and me. No one was catching fish. Anthony got a bite and Frank helped him bring it in. He was showing him how to reel it in. About five minutes later, Anthony got another bite. Frank said, "Tony, the fish is taking your son next to the water."

I was putting a worm on my hook and got the hook in my finger. I dropped my pole and ran to my son but Frank had him just as his feet got into the water. It was a five-pound sucker. We gave the fish to Frank and then Frank got the fishhook out of my finger. This man, Frank, was a wonderful man, a true gentleman. This is a true fish story.

Out on Lake Erie with my thirteen foot boat and getting ready to do some fishing, I got up to throw my anchor out and this powerful motorboat came about fifteen feet from me. The Wake made me fall and I lost a beautiful surfing rod. The anchor fell on my big toe of my right foot. Through the years, I had to have my nail removed; now I don't have any nail on that big toe.

One other time, I floated down a very fast creek that ran into Lake Erie. I was out about two miles into the lake and the white caps started to form. Lake Erie, not being a deep lake, the waves get up fast so I started to put gas in my motor. It's not easy when the water is acting up. I didn't get enough gas in the tank so I started back when I hit something and broke the propeller pin. The waves were now rougher, and with no motor I had a good distance to row. The best I could do was to turn the bow into the waves and use the oars to keep the little boat facing the waves. I felt safe due to my lifejacket. If I did get swamped, the water would push me to shore.

I knew I was losing ground because the shoreline was getting closer. Forcing the bow into the waves, I finally got beached and nowhere to go. The next wave swamped the boat; it filled with water.

High on a hill a lady was watching from her window with her two sons. When I climbed out of the boat her two sons were there and said that their mother wanted me to come to the house and dry out. We tipped the boat over to get the water out and dragged the boat up on the shore. When I got to the house, I didn't want to go in. This was a beautiful home with plush carpets. She said to come in and not to worry about getting things wet. I asked her where I was, and she said on a private beach in Angola. I explained what happened and she couldn't believe it. I had gone all that distance without a motor and just my oars. She said that was about twenty-five miles away. She had been watching me for the last twenty minutes, and she was planning to send her boys after me if I lost control. I made a phone call to get a ride and picked up my boat three days later, and thanked the lady and her sons for their kindness.

In 1964, when I was in the National Guard, my wife and children went on vacation with me. I was in full uniform and got full discounts on any place we went. I believe we were at the Holiday Inn, fifty miles from Washington D.C. There were no rooms available but the desk clerk got the maids and porters to clean up the special room. It was ours for the next three nights at a great discount. All I had to do was drive the fifty miles to get there.

While in the city, we went to Arlington Cemetery and the Tomb of the Unknown Soldier. They were just going to change the guard. The Marine Sergeant came up to me and asked if I would join them in a salute as a soldier since I was in uniform. What an honor that was.

When I was thirty-nine years old, I joined the National Guard. The First Sergeant said," Why don't you get into the Post Office. You are a ten-point veteran and you can have an open exam. I took his advice and passed the test. Again, I was given a hard time by the personnel due to my nervous problem. I said, "If I don't get the job, I will go to the newspaper." I was told that I had to go to my doctor and be back in twenty hours or lose the job. I saw my doctor and was back in five hours; the job was mine.

I was promoted to Corporal when my World War II records were checked. They found I was awarded the Bronze Star twenty years ago and the State of New York gave me the New York State Conspicuous Service Cross, based on the Bronze Star. When the award was given to me my wife and children, the whole battalion was out as well as the newspaper reporters. I was on the front page. In the meantime at the post office, two janitors and me had twenty-eight stations to clean up. By the time you finished the last one, you started all over again.

At the National Guard, I was chosen to go to the Empire State Academy that was run by West Point officers. This was the first time I was away from my wife in seventeen years. I was out of the service for twenty years. Reporting to the Acting First Sergeant, I had to read a sign that I couldn't see clearly so I turned my head so I could see the sign better. He said, "Read it without turning your head."

I said, "I can't read it without turning."

"Step outside," he said.

Just as we stepped outside, another soldier ran by without saluting him. The LT told me to do ten push-ups with my rifle across the backside of my hands. I was pumping away. I got up to sixty.

The LT yelled, "Ten."

"I thought you meant a hundred." I was told to get up. Now it was the other soldiers turn and he could not go beyond five.

"This soldier is forty-years-old and you can't do ten?" the LT growled. "Report to me after chow."

We had to fall out in full uniform and the Acting First Sergeant came to our barracks and saw me. "What are you doing with all them medals and the combat infantry badge and the Bronze Star? Take them off."

"I will not, and you better not try." I stood my ground.

"Then first report to the Officer in Charge."

"Now?"

The First Sergeant was out of New York City outfit and didn't know me. The officer that made me do the push-ups came to me and said that I was going to be in every field trail. I knew what to expect. These weekend soldiers knew nothing of night combat problems. One night problem we had to go into an enemy area and was told the enemy is green berets. This was a very dark night and the soldiers were scared with shells going off and shooting. I led every patrol, telling each man to remember who is behind you and who is in front of you because the enemy will try to creep in. I managed to spot three of the enemy before they spotted me, calling out: "You are shot. You are dead." I got through without being spotted.

The next night we had to attack a mountain ridge; the enemy was on the other side. The Captain asked, "How are we going to take this mountain?"

I said, "By a three prong attack; one platoon in a frontal attack and two flanking attacks." Each soldier set his watch with mine --- ten minutes to get into position. The frontal unit would go up to get in their position and ten minutes later the other two units should go into attack and catch them off guard. And again I was lucky. I captured the officer in charge.

The following day we had a whole battalion march and I was told I didn't have to march. That evening, the First LT came to me and said the Colonel wanted to see me. I was puzzled. Did I hurt someone in one of our attacks? As I entered the officer's quarters, there was the Colonel, a Captain, and the West Point officer. I saluted them. The Corporal told me to relax and sit down. Now I was really puzzled.

The Captain spoke first, "I liked how you attacked that mountain from three sides and had the soldiers set their watches with yours and surprise the enemy."

The Colonel spoke next: "You were told you did not have to march on your bad ankle and yet you put yourself at the end of the column and marched with your men. Next year I would like you to come back as Acting First Sergeant and go to OCS to become an officer."

"I am over 40 years old," I said, "and OCS is over by your twenty-eighth birthday. That would be a no-no."

"We can take care of that and bypass Second Louie and be a First LT," he said.

I went home and told my wife that they want me to be an officer. I was on "cloud nine". It didn't take more than five minutes and my wife burst my bubble, and said, "Don't you see why they want to cut through all that red tape? They are going to send you to the Far East and you got a bad leg. You don't see that do you?"

"Not until right now," I said. My year was up and my leg wasn't any better and I did not sign up again.

I rented a boat with my wife, brother-in-law and my wife's sister. We were out about fifteen minutes when the motor fell off in a fast, muddy river. I was going to jump in after it and my brother-in-law yelled, "There are undertows in this part and you won't be able to see it. Let's go back. I will take your car out of the lot while you go talk to the manager."

When I got there, there was a State police officer. I told the manager that the motor was not secured right but he tried to blame us. "We didn't even have to come back to tell you," I protested.

The officer said, "One look at you, I could find you anywhere."

"How could you find me when you didn't even know what I looked like?"

The manager said, "You'll have to pay for the motor."

"I'll pay my share for what a used motor would cost."

My brother-in-law didn't pay anything. He went to see a lawyer friend. We tried to resolve this. The manager was real nasty. I told him some day you are going to have a problem. About two months later his son got killed in a car accident.

One day my wife, nephew, niece and me went bowling. The place was packed. There was a trophy for high score and low score. My wife, who had never bowled before, started to get strikes. We didn't get high score but almost lost low score. The owner was going to give it to his friends. My nephew, in a very loud voice, said, "My Aunt and Uncle are the low score champions." And we were; we got the trophy.

When the price of meat was high I raised rabbits and had a brother-in-law kill them. I could not kill anything that I raised. I had to give one kill to my brother-in-law every time. We also had a nice garden. My son's godparents came to our place and I told them that they could pick some items out of the garden. To my surprise they picked the garden clean. I didn't know this until after they left.

I was going hunting with my brother-in-law, John, and his brother. He fired his gun when his barrel was close to my face; I could feel the blast. He shot at the same rabbit five times. The dog kept chasing the rabbit then gave up, and just sat the next time he fired. Going deer hunting was just as bad. A deer was spotted. John's brother yelled, and the deer jumped as I fired. He told me he could see the bullet hit the deer. The deer was about 500 yards away. I never went hunting with them again. The next year, my brother-in-law shot himself. I wasn't there. He tripped and the gun went off and shot himself in his hand. He ran with the safety off.

My brother-in-law's mother was in the hospital. I called Marty to come over fast, your mother is dying. She was a sweet, old Italian lady and could not speak English. She stayed with the Italian ways. Most of the Italians that came over stuck to their ways and stayed together. They enjoyed the freedom of America yet stayed with the customs of Italy. We called it Little Italy, all hard working people. I called Marty again and he said he had to finish shaving. I stayed by her side. I always joked with her. Every time I had visited, I would ask her for a kiss in Italian. It was one of the few words I knew. She always got a big kick out of this. And she would tell my wife that I was a nice wolf in Italian, and laugh. At her bedside, I asked her one more time for the kiss and I kissed her. I got the most beautiful smile; and she died in my arms and went to heaven. She would always come to me and knew I didn't understand Italian, the few words I knew, and spend time with her. She really enjoyed my company. Marty was late; his mother was gone. We were glad she didn't die alone.

One day I had my sister, Frances, her girlfriend and my son on a boat ride. We were out for hours. The only shade was covering my son from the blazing sun. We got burned from a combination of the direct sun and the reflection off the water. He was the only one not burned. I lost three days work. My sister's girlfriend, who had a very light complexion and a red head, got burned the most. My wife and I went to see her. She was not wearing any clothes. All she had on was a big bath towel holding it up in front of her so we could not see her body. After about fifteen minutes she said we had to leave. She couldn't hold the towel up much longer. We had to laugh and we left.

Another time, I went hunting with my brother. He had a BB gun. I shot a pheasant; it dropped and started to run. I shot it again. It fell over and got up and started to run. Then it stopped and turned to look at me. I couldn't shoot. My brother ran up and knocked its head off with the stock of the BB gun. I could not eat anything that I killed. My mother cooked it and they ate it.

On another boat ride with my brother, Bob, we got back to the dock. I walked to the inside of my boat to raise the motor up to my brother but the boat moved and I fell in the water with the motor. My brother was laughing; I was kicking and swearing that I was going to lose the motor.

My brother said, "You're in two feet of water and you got a life jacket." He laughed even harder.

There was a priest standing nearby, and he said I shouldn't swear like that. I don't recall what I said to him but I know I didn't swear at him.

I remember one day my father-in-law gave me his double-barreled shotgun to get rid of the wild birds in his grapes. I did and gave the birds to my mother-in-law and told her that some of those birds were not wild. "I could get in a lot of trouble," I told her. "Tell your husband you can't just shoot them because they're on your property." When I pulled the trigger, I forgot it was a double-barrel, and pulled both triggers at the same time – I got a good kick.

The next day state police officers asked my mother-in-law if she saw anybody shooting. She said, "I no hear any guns." While they were speaking, the birds were being cooked in tomato sauce.

I got a letter from my father's brother, also named Anthony. He said that his sister just moved to Ohio from Italy. I could not go there at the time but the following year my wife, my mother and our two children traveled there by way of Pennsylvania. Through the mountains of Pennsylvania, this driver cut me off so sharp that we almost went over a cliff. I started after him and I was about fifty feet behind him. I was going to beat the hell out of him or cut him short. I believe he knew it; he kept looking back, and then I saw a child. I slowed down and gave up the chase.

As we were driving on, a tornado was going the same way that we were but cut a path a few miles to my right. It seemed that even with my car, I told my wife that I didn't know how wide of a problem it could be, so I sped up to 65 miles an hour.

I felt a gust of wind tear at us. My son said, "Dad, there is a building in the air following us."

I gave it the gas to ninety miles an hour and the building fell about twenty-five feet behind us. It was one of those small information booths. Thanks to our son letting us know about the building following us, we were able to avoid an accident. I believe that if it hit us we might not be here.

We arrived in Ohio and went to the address; no Aunt. I asked around and all I found out was that she had married shoemaker. I went to the police station to see what I could find out. I was told that he sold his business and moved back to Italy. I never heard from them again.

On our way back, I got lost on a wrong street and a police officer figures that I was lost and he came to me. He was a great help and very polite. I felt bad that I didn't get his name so I could send him a letter and thank him.

I was picking my wife up from work one afternoon. As we approached the stoplight, it had turned green for me to go forward. I was making a left turn and there were two cars parked on the approaching left lane waiting for their light to turn green. Another car came into the oncoming lane to get around the two cars and he hit me. If I had been another two feet forward, he would have hit me dead center on my door.

The police questioned the driver and the driver claimed that he wasn't speeding.

The officer asked him where he worked, was it the end of his shift, and what time did he punch out. From what he gathered, the officer said that he could not get to this point of the accident unless he was going over eighty miles an hour.

He could have killed us. We won the case.

When my wife worked at American Machine Foundry, there was a big rainstorm. I drove my wife to work with her girlfriend. Under the bridge, the road had flooded. I had to push my car on one side of the lane so I put my fishing boots on. I walked through the water and carried each gal on my back to the car.

Chapter Five
My Golden Years in California

We arrived in California in January of 1966. We left a completely remodeled home with a two-car garage under the house, a laundry room and a workshop. We rented the two and a half story for $85 dollars a month. I had eighteen thousand invested in the house. A little later, I will tell you more about this house and the renters.

The first month, we stayed at my brother-in-law's house and we shared in the groceries. We found a house for sale a few blocks away and the owner wanted $18,000 dollars. The neighbor next door offered him $19,000 dollars. He refused the offer, saying, "You need a house better than your neighbor and you only have a thousand dollars to put down. I will take the second for $30 dollars per month."

The house was now ours. Every once in awhile he would say, "If you can't make ends meet, it's all right. You can catch up at the end." We met every payment on time. I took out a policy with the bank, in case of disability the payments would be met. I had also taken out a policy with an insurance company. If I got hurt and couldn't work, I would get $400 per month. Best thing I ever did. I always believed in insurance.

In 1968, we put in a ground pool for about $2,500 dollars. Then I got a letter from my tenant that something went wrong with the brand new furnace. He sent only half of his payment. That was in 1967 and again in 1968, I put the house up for sale for $18,500 dollars, and it won't sell. I kept lowering the price and it still won't sell. So I had my sister send someone over to look at the house as if they might want to buy it. The tenant said the roof leaked and it was a new roof. He said that the furnace kept breaking down but it was anew furnace. All of this information was taken to a lawyer. If the tenant didn't get out within thirty days, he was going to be sued; he left. Here he had a completely remodeled house for only $85 dollars a month. He didn't want to move. I sold the house for $11,500 dollars, a big loss. He also stole all of the copper pipe I had and some other items. I was too far away to do anything and he knew it.

Now getting back to my house in Reseda, California; I had a third bathroom put in at the master bathroom and a door that you could go to the pool. I also had a fireplace and a 25 by 30 foot room with two sliding doors that you could go directly to the pool. I also built a bar.

Suddenly the contractor took me to court for more money because he had to order more cement to finish the job. He came to me and said, "I need more money for cement because I can't finish the job."

"You can't leave it like that, this is part of the room."

So he went and ordered more cement and I wouldn't pay him. This was unacceptable and he decided to sue. When we went to court he had a law book. He was going to tell the judge the law. I found out that three other homeowners were also suing him. I had all of my plans and the layouts where I wanted the cement work done plus I had to call the building inspector that the fireplace chimney wasn't high enough. I also told the judge that they were cleaning all there cement tools in my pool. I was ready for the battle.

The judge told me to take him to court on the damages to the pool. My wife didn't want to do it. As it turned out, this contractor lost all the court cases; and, standing outside the court building, he said the judge didn't know the law.

Our pool provided our family with good memories. But there was one time that wasn't. I had my wife take swimming lessons and she learned to swim very well. She could even float on her back, which I could not do. We were all swimming one afternoon when my wife decided to get out of the pool at the deep end. She grabbed for the deck but instead she grabbed a small water float and fell backward and panicked. I went to her and she started to fight me.

"I am going to do the Deadman's Float and you grab me and crawl out of the pool over my body." She scratched the hell out of me. I called my son, who was a Seal in the Navy, and he came to help.

She turned on him and grabbed the top of his head and pushed him under the water. He got away and came up behind her with a rescue hold so he could take her down to the shallow end. Our son's swimming skills saved his mother.

We were having trouble with yellow jackets while we were swimming. I got stung twice at the same time. I knew that the yellow jackets were getting water to mix with mud to make their nests. After getting nailed twice, a war began between the wasps and me. I got a two-by-four and cut it down to a two-by-two. I smoothed one end to fit my hand and on the other end nailed a twelve-by-twelve piece of plywood to it. Now I was ready for war with my new bee swatter. You guessed it; I won the war. That was the end of the yellow jackets. Even with all of our fruit trees, the regular bees never became a problem.

When I made the earlier trip to California, I did it in fifty-four hours. It took me days to feel like myself again. My new job at Van Nuys Post Office was loading and unloading 40-foot trailers with eighty-pound mailbags. When there were no trucks, we pulled full mail sacks and got them ready to be shipped out. We also would get mail from other trucks that would come down a conveyor belt. You had to read the label and make sure it got on the right hand truck. We also hung sacks for the clerks so they could throw their mail, pull away full tubs of mail, and sort mail on the belts. It was all hard work.

I helped on a Mark 2 belt that cancelled the stamps. Later I bid on the job of doing repair, and got it. Sometimes the machine broke down and I would repair it, mostly on weekends. I was the only Mark 2 operator that knew how to fix them. I continued that job for about five years.

My wife and I dropped off our son off at work, and on the way back were stopped in traffic for a red light. I looked in the driver's rear mirror and saw a car coming too fast. That driver was looking out her side window, not paying attention to traffic.

Inside the car in front of me, I could see a little boy standing up looking out of the back window. I knew I was going to be hit so I pressed hard on my brake so my car would not go forward, hit their car and hurt the little boy.

My foot on the brake was like the car hitting a street pole. The impact went right up to my back. The lady told me she was looking across at the storefronts and didn't notice that the cars were stopping for a red light. She tried to change her story.

For me, I was grateful to avoid the car ahead of us. After many treatments on my back pain that were not helping, I had to go for a back fusion. They gave me eight pints of blood. My wife and daughter said that I gave up because of the pain. My daughter said something to me and I got mad and perked up. Until this day I don't know what she said. I was in the hospital for thirty days and refused pain shots because they gave me very bad headaches.

I had a full body cast with a hole cut out in the middle. After those thirty days in the hospital, I went home and put a pillow under me and I felt something odd. We went back to the doctor for an x-ray. He found that I had cracked part of the fusion. The doctor said it might fuse itself again, so I went back home and recuperated.

I was home almost a year and the Postmaster said that if I was gone a year, I wold lose all my rights and benefits. So two days before my year was up, I went back to work with the cracked fusion. I was back on the Mark 2 canceling machine. I was the first Mark 2 operator to get a superior performance and a $250 dollar check in which Uncle Sam wanted his $50 dollars.

I was on that machine for a whole year with the cracked fusion. My doctor told me that I got hepatitis C from the blood transfusion and that I didn't have a normal brain wave. He said it might be due to all of the machines in the hospital. I haven't had another one to find out. It might not be normal but it's working fine.

It was now time for the second spinal fusion since the crack didn't mend. This time I had to have three pints of blood.

I was home for three months, then returned to work. I went into security. I had taken many management tests including Second Class Postmaster, Public Relations, and passed every one of them.

I was acting Forman of Mails and had a better production rate than the full-time foremen of mails. The General Foreman gave me high marks and said that I would make foreman. The lady superintendent didn't like me, and said, "Set him down."

So I went back to security. The reason why the super didn't like me was that she wanted the black man to go for security but I had military service background and more seniority.

She came to me, "I didn't think you knew about guns."

"I am an Italian; our teething ring was a gun."

No one liked her.

I was at the security desk and this gentleman came in. I got up and said, "May I help you?"

"I am the new Postmaster." He introduced the men with him to me. The old Postmaster would pass you and never say a word, or if a stranger came into the building, he would never tell us who they were.

After a few weeks, he came up to me and said, "You were up for supervisor. What happened?"

I told him, and he said, "I feel the same way here, sort of a cold feeling. Am I right?"

I smiled. I told him who wanted the job, about the superintendent, and the general foreman, and so on. Next thing I knew, I was back on the floor as an acting foreman. I stayed a few months and found out I was losing money and being there longer than eight hours, so I stepped down and went back to security.

The superintendent was shipped out to a distant town as supervisor. The general foreman was shipped out and he quit. The one that wanted the Postmaster position was shipped to a station as a Postmaster. So all of the people who gave me a problem and the Postmaster a problem were gone. About a year later, the Postmaster came to me and said his wife didn't like it here and they were going back to Utah.

My friend, George, and I used to go to the Los Angeles Forest creek panning for gold. We found fool's gold and a pain in the back. We had metal detectors and went into old gold mine tunnels. We would get a ton of newspapers wrapped around our legs in case of rattlesnakes and black widow spiders. We carried a torch so we could burn the spider webs.

This one day, my machine started to buzz like hell so we dug it out. It was a round rock about five pounds. Now I carried this all day and I was in a full body cast due to my spinal fusion. When we got home, we got a hammer and broke the rock and felt bad; the dead center was iron ore. No gold.

One other time, George and I and a desert rat decided to go to the Pacific Ocean near Malibu. We had our detectors and mine started to go crazy again. I was still in my full body cast that would not let me bend or dig, so George and this old rat started to dig. Two feet down the machine was now louder. I got up closer and some dirt started to fall into the hole and I was told to move back. The digging was now four or five feet, and I started to move forward again and once more told to stay back.

Now we all thought it might be a ship's anchor. About six feet down we saw silver like metal. It was two or three feet around. It was the drainpipe that came from the other side of the highway to our digging.

"Boy, we did a lot of digging to find nothing, "I said glumly."

Their remark was: "What do you mean 'we'. I think we are going to put you in that hole with your machine."

I started to laugh. From that day on we just scanned the beaches and parks.

My wife worked at Rockedyne factory and then at RCA. Our son enlisted in the Navy and went to Vietnam. It was a hard time for my wife. My son would write to me at the post office and write to his mother.

My wife woke up one night and said that Anthony just got hurt and she was right. His letter came to me confirming it. I got a shot of penicillin. As I was leaving the doctor's office, I started losing my balance and went to the floor. People's faces were getting bigger. I was picked up and carried to the far office in a backroom and laid on a table. The doctor asked his nurse if she had any candy. She offered me a Hershey bar.

I felt close to death. I kept saying to myself: "I can't die now, my son is in Vietnam and if I die my wife is going to go to pieces. She's close to a nervous breakdown with our son away." I survived one more time --- it wasn't my time yet.

On February 9th, 1971, my wife was out of bed to go to work. She was making coffee in the kitchen and I was sleeping. All at once, I heard a scream. "Tony, we are having an earthquake."

"Wait. I have to put my pants on," I yelled.

The house was still shaking. The pool water was splashing out of the pool and the wine bottles fell off the bar shelves and broke. After things settled down, I went and started the car and took my wife to work. When we got there they sent everybody back home. Just walking in the room you would get drunk; the smell of wine was so bad. A wino would love it.

In security, I was the only officer that carried a gun. We were all called watchmen out of the mail handler craft. This was Level Four and if you were called security they would have to put you in a higher grade five. Once a year we would have to go to Los Angeles for training on our weapons. My scores were so high that they were often higher than the postal inspectors that fired every three months.

There was one time we had pop-up targets. You would have to put two bullets in each target in six seconds; I would do it in four seconds. The Sergeant called a lot of the LA security men to see me shoot. I carried my .357 as my sidepiece.

I was on armed action when a letter was sent to our office with two armed, security men. It was handed to a carrier and I was called to go with him. The envelope had over $400 dollars of postage in it. We delivered it to Burbank but found no such address, and we made a call to North Hollywood. No such person. A general foreman was calling us to come back. The letter was turned into the safe until they called Los Angeles Security Police.

I rode on trucks that carried thousands of dollars in postage. When post office boxes were blown up, I was the one that they sent. One time a Vietnam veteran called up and said he was coming in to shoot the acting female supervisor. I was told to meet him. He came on a motorcycle and tried to enter through a narrow walkway gate and I stopped him.

My first words were: "Are you a veteran?"

He said, "Yes."

"So am I. Now you can be in a lot of trouble," while I said this I unzipped my jacket. "You are subject to five years in jail and a $5000 dollar fine, when you called and said you were going to hurt a federal employee." I saw him think it over. "I am now going to open your saddlebags and pat you down, and I will let you go."

He gave me no trouble. We also found out later that he had no home address.

When checking the Encino Post Office, I smelled smoke and could not see any fire. I opened the office door and the smoke was a little stronger, and still saw no fire. I went back into the mailroom and the smoke was coming from a wastebasket. I put it out and called the fire department. Whenever there was smoke or fire the fire department must be called.

I was called to check a post office that all the outside doors were open. Two supervisors went with me. After I cleared the office, they were to see if everything was in order. I told both of the supervisors to wait outside. If I ran into trouble they should get out and call the police. I drew my gun and went in one of the doors and started looking behind the mail cases. Here came the younger supervisor around a case. He went through the other door. I said, 'You dumb ass, didn't I tell you to wait outside. You are lucky I am not trigger-happy. You would have been a dead dumb ass." I was really pissed.

There were a few guys on their break in their cars drinking beer --- the hippie type. One guy threw an empty can at me. I went over to the car and I knew who the leader was because I talked to him at different times, just small talk.

"Blondie, you seem to be the leader here. Did I ever say anything to you or the guys out here about drinking?"

"No," he said.

"Well, as long as you stayed in your cars, I said nothing. I figure that if your supervisor didn't care about smelling beer on you and didn't miss you, that's his problem. One of you assholes threw an empty can at me. If you want to enjoy your beer while you are here on break, you all better calm down and drink like a mouse because I can turn all of you in because you are not supposed to be out here on break."

One of the smart asses asked, "Can you shoot?"

"If you're the one that threw that can, I can dot an 'i' right between your eyes at seventy-five feet. You want to find out, just try me."

Blondie spoke up. "There is talk that he's the best shot of all LA Postal Officers. Don't let his size fool you."

I never had a problem with my size or with them after this.

One day my wife and her sister and husband went to Big Bear Lake with me. We traveled a dirt road to check where an old gold mine used to be. There was a lot of snow and ruts in the road. I had a front-wheel drive Olds Tornado and had no problem going to the mine. On the way back, some jerk was coming with a small pick-up and lost control because he was going too fast. He headed for me. I steered to the left and got into a big rut where someone else must have gotten stuck.

I told everyone to just be calm and I would get them out there. "First, I am going to check the front end," I told them.

My brother-in-law asked for gum and he didn't even chew gum. He was as nervous as a cat. I asked him to check the front wheels on the passenger side while I checked my side.

He said, "We are about ten or twelve feet from going over the cliff."

"We are backing up. We are not going forward and front-wheel drive will drive us out. Just sit on the front fender on the passenger side to give it a little weight. This way you can jump off if there is any trouble." I put it in reverse and pulled out.

He and his wife asked for more gum.

Another time while on security for the post office, I was walking between parked cars and I saw someone seated in a car. I walked up real slow and I used my flashlight with a red cone on the end. As I was watching, he had a spoon in his hand and was putting a lit match under it. Just at that moment, I put the flashlight on him. The spoon went up in the air and he lost whatever was in that spoon.

He said that he thought I was a cop with that red flashlight. I told him, "You were going to take that dope. You can be fired for that."

"Are you going to turn me in?"

"No, because I didn't see you take it but you are going to sign yourself up for a class that the post office is giving. If you don't, I will put you on report. And I'll check up on you."

When he got out of the car and I walked him to the door, he said, "If anyone gives you any trouble or problems, let me know because I am going to tell the brothers that you are an okay guy."

I was locking a post office building and when walked toward the government car, three men ran away from it. When I got to the car, I saw a five-gallon can of gas that they siphoned out. I put the five-gallon can in the back seat and got in the car. Two of the men came back. The tall skinny man wanted his gas can back.

"I can't give you your can because it has my gas in it," I told them.

The tall heavier guy said nothing but the skinny guy said, "If you didn't have that gun on you, we would take the gas and beat the hell out of you."

"You guys are really dumb. You came back so I can identify you, and then he admits it's his can," I said to the big guy in disbelief. "If he keeps it up I am going to get out of this car and shoot you because you are bigger than the loudmouth."

They left. I would never have shot my gun with gas fumes and a five-gallon can of gas in my car but the dummies wouldn't have known that. I had no way to get in touch with the main office. I was told to give up the gun because they were afraid that if I used it the post office would be sued. I said, "You don't give a damn if I got beat or left for dead, as long as the post office wasn't sued."

I got off the 28-station security run and stayed at the main office. I kept a jacket on all the time, this way the employees didn't know if I had a gun on me or not. The outside dopers would drive in and dump something in the garage cans and leave. I would turn this information in to an L.A. Postal Inspector and they would call me at home or come to my home. One supervisor was putting me in for a Superior Performance Award but he got cancer and died soon after. He was the only one that knew what was going on. He always thought I was carrying a gun under my jacket.

I had a lot of problems, too many to mention. The last one before I left the post office was about another veteran, who was having an affair with an employee's wife. He even went to her home and beat up her husband. He came to the post office to beat up the husband again. A supervisor escorted him outside and called me.

The supervisor told him to get in the car, "Tony will take you home. "

I opened the door and told him to get in the front seat.

He told me, "You're not big enough to put me in the front seat."

I figured that I got a problem here. I looked at him and said, "We can do it the easy way or the hard way. It's up to you. It makes no difference to me." I guess he thought I was going to back off. He got in the car.

About three blocks away, a police car appeared. He said, "Tony, you got the authority, not them. Just get me home."

I did and about five months later I went on sick leave.

I was having problems with my upper back since World War II. I kept getting pain in my chest area that doctors thought it might be my heart so I was given an angioplasty. All went well other than having hearing problems, high blood pressure, and stomach problems. Life is fine. After all, it's the "golden years". My Uncle Walter always said that doctors have to get into your wallets --- how else can they buy their cars and boats?

I was working in my workshop. It was time to clean and oil my floor model band saw. I had taken the top cover off to clean the sawdust out and line up the circular saw blade. I bent down to oil the bottom and reached over to pull myself up and grabbed the moving blade. I was lucky that the blade cut only my little finger down the length of the finger, otherwise I would have lost my finger. I turned the machine off, wrapped a cloth around the finger, and went to the house. I asked my wife to make a bandage with tape to keep my finger together then I drove to the hospital and got a few stitches. At times the finger feels funny but it works good, and makes a good ear cleaner.

Another time, I was cleaning plaster off a board near the bathroom tub. My foot slipped and the utility knife went into my left wrist. Lucky one more time that the knife didn't hit the ulna or main nerves. I could have been in a lot of trouble.

In the last few years, we've had a couple of large earthquakes in Big Bear as we sat in our house, you could see the walls move. It makes us think about longevity.

On February 10th, 2003, death was at my door again. I was given a medicine called a Clondine pill and it gave me pain in the chest. I told the doctor and he didn't believe it. I was already on Atenolol pills so he added Norvasec and on top of this he gave me Nitroglycerin capsules to take twice a day. He ordered another nitro to put under the tongue. I am glad I didn't order the nitro pill. If I did, I wouldn't be writing my own story.

While I was eating with my wife, she said that my eyes started to roll and I passed out and fell to the floor. I believe it was my wife screaming that brought me to. My wife called a neighbor for help. She gave me a glass of Seven-Up and I felt okay. The phone rang and I got up to answer it. My brother, Lewis, was on the phone telling me that my youngest sister's husband had died. I turned to tell my wife and she said, "What are you doing on the floor?"

I had passed out. Again the paramedics were called. One hospital was not taking any emergency patients because they were full. I was in another hospital for a day and a half in their emergency room before I was able to get a room. The emergency room doctor told me to change doctors, which I did.

For awhile, I also worked part-time for U/S Guard as armed security on a twenty-eight acre Nike Base high in the L.A. Hills. One night I had my little Doxie, Brownie, with me, and she started barking. I looked out the window and saw nothing. I had a good view to the street about 1500 feet away, and a very high fence.

We had many little buildings that we would have to go check and punch a clock. So when Brownie wouldn't stop barking I knew she was trying to tell me something. I lifted my gun out of my holster and opened the door.

Brownie flew out of the door running. I looked up to see where she was going. And there, on a far fence, a mountain lion. The lion was facing our way. I yelled at Brownie to stop. She stopped at the same time that I fired my gun into the ground. In one jump that lion cleared the fence and was gone.

I walked to the fence and flashed my light in that area and fired once more into the ground and then reloaded my pistol. It was time to check the little building so I got my clock and told Brownie to come along. I flashed every building to make sure there were no lions on the roofs.

The next day, I brought my .12 gauge shotgun with double-ought shell and my .357 and my German Shepherd. I followed the lion's tracks and they were about ten feet from the door. He must have smelled my dog and when he heard me talking to Brownie, he left. I believe if I didn't have my dog, I would have been lion meat. The job ended when U/S Guard lost its contract and they got their own security men.

We sold our home in Reseda and bought a twenty-seven foot trailer and placed it in a trailer park in Van Nuys. We bought an acre and a quarter lot in Lucerne Valley, California and had a custom-built house constructed. When the house was finished, I had a foreman pull my trailer to Lucerne Valley. He placed it under three large trees. My wife lived in the trailer for a month while the house was being finished. I slept in my pick-up at the post office or some park and then at my daughter's place about twenty miles away.

I went to Lucerne Valley on weekends. I worked all night, drove one hundred and ten miles, ate breakfast and started cutting down trees and trimming the rest. This went on from

June to December of 1984. I was dog-tired working all night and Saturday and Sunday on our land.

It was about 2 a.m. and it started to rain and lightning. My wife woke me up because she was scared of being under the trees. I told her to go to sleep, that I was tired. She woke me up again and said that the pick-up wasn't big enough to pull the trailer.

I said, "Go to sleep."

She woke me up again, and said, "Move the truck so we can get out of here if something happens."

I got up and turned the truck so we could drive out if we had to, then I dragged myself to bed.

She woke me again. I said, "I work all week, drove 110 miles to get home and worked these last two days that I was here. I am dog-tired. If the lightning hits the propane tanks you won't know what happened, so go to sleep." Morning came and all was well.

When we moved here in 1984, we were told about the rattlesnakes and especially the Mojave Greens. The Mojaves are more dangerous than the Diamond backs. In the month of July in 1985, I was cutting the grass. I went to the water faucet to wash my hands in the five-gallon bucket. My hand was about six inches from the bucket. Boy, did I jump. There was a snake drinking from the bucket. I got my pistol that was near by for this reason in case a snake was close.

This snake was fast up the tree and down because it knew I was after it. I could not run as fast as that snake moved. I shot it. It was five feet and seven inches long. I was told it was not a poisonous snake; it was a gopher snake. They kill Mojaves and standard rattlesnakes. In all of our years here, we have never come across a poisonous snake.

My wife moved into our new house in July of 1984 and by December 1984 is when I went out on sick leave. My retirement was May 31st of 1985. My brother-in-law and I put in steel fence posts and hung three hundred and thirty feet of five-foot fencing on the north side of the property. My wife and I put up one hundred and five feet of fencing and two wide gates in front on the west side. In the meantime, we were getting tons of stones to dress up the front yard and our circular driveway.

I got another job as a security guard at a casino in Adelanto. At the casino for their New Year's Eve party they hired a big black man for back up. My wife was there for New Year's Eve. A lumberman came in with a big knife on his belt and you just can't go to the card tables with any kind of weapon. The stand-by security was scared to go ask for the knife. I went to the man and said, "Sir, your knife, please. It will be returned to you when you leave." I got the knife and the guard was fired.

One night on closing the bar, I had to see that everyone left. One guy refused, and asked me, "Do you know how to use that club? I can take it away from you."

"No," I said, "I use it as a toothpick. Do you need some teeth picked?"

There was another black security guard. He was all right. He was standing about twenty-five feet away and just watching, standing there, and laughing and shaking his head. I was carrying a PR 24, a club that you can spin with a side handle.

There were three men; one was about to walk out the door with a glassful of liquor. I said, "Sir, you are not allowed to go outside with that glass."

"Really," he said. His other friends stood by the wall with big grins on their faces. I figured it was a test. I said, "Sir, that's a lot of booze in that glass. Did you ever chug-a-lug with that much booze in a glass?"

"Sure," he said. "Easy."

I just started to smile. People say they can but they often can't. He poured it down with one gulp. "Now, you don't need the glass," I said.

He handed it to me. The other two men started laughing their heads off. The guy that I was confronting said, " You are a smooth one. If anybody gives you trouble just call me. Here is my card." And he gave me a pen. I shook hands with them and they left.

I was always called when the armored car came in. Harley motorcycle riders came in one time, and they looked me up and said if there was any trouble to call them. There was one card player, an Oriental dealer, who said to me, "I can take that club from you. I am a black belt."

I said, "What degree?" But he didn't answer. "I'm a six degreed black belt. Do you still think you can take it away from me? You are welcome to try." I am not any kind of black belt but he didn't challenge me.

I worked there for a few months but the smoke from the heavy smokers was hanging on my clothes and I was bringing the smell home. I had some big projects to do: install a sprinkler system, plant grass, install watering timers, build some storage buildings --- a lot of work. I bought a riding lawnmower, a tractor, another chain saw, and a floor model table saw.

One of the first things after we moved in was to dig out a big twenty-foot tree that was in front of the house. After it was dug out, we dragged it about twenty-five feet and let it lay there for about a week. We dug another deep hole and with help we got the tree in the new hole. Now twenty years later, it's doing fine.

Next we had to clear the yard behind the house. We hired a man with a tractor and plow to dig the asparagus out and level the area. My wife and I dug over seven hundred feet of trench to lay our PVC pipe, many electric and anti-siphon valves, two timers, and many, many sprinkler heads. Then we planted thirty fruit trees. Years later they all died except for the pomegranate tree.

The grass is growing and so is my water bill. I then had a spa put in. The next project was a workshop, so I built a nine-by-twenty building with a lean-to for junk. The next project was a ten-by-ten storage shed. Now my wife wanted a gazebo. I needed to enclose the spa with a roof and use T-111 paneling for the bottom and lattice for the upper sides.

I then extended the roof another twenty feet for a carport using four-by-fours as supports. I build two rows of cement blocks to stop some of the sand from blowing into the yard. The six-ton of rock that I had put down was already covered. I had a twenty-ton truck remove sand from my front fence.

While I was putting the rolled roofing on the carport roof, I had an empty five-gallon can of tar cement. As I let it go, my wife walked out from under the carport and the can fell on her head. Why she walked under the carport instead of the side walkway I will never know. I got down real fast. I could do nothing; my hands were full of tar. I cleaned my hands to some degree and rushed her to the fire department. They cleaned the area up as best they could and took my wife to the hospital. She got eight stitches.

We went to Big Bear Lake for a visit and to help chop a tree down. I went to get a rope to pull it down and this guy gave it another chop and the tree fell on my head and sat me down. I mentioned earlier that my brain wave was not normal; this is when the doctor told me this.

Another time, we were returning from Big Bear after getting wood for our fireplace, when my breaks went out on my Toyota pick-up. Coming down this winding mountain road with sharp curves that snaked all the way to the desert floor was horrifying for us. Talk about a wild ride; this was it. With every snake like curve was a deep severe drop. We would all be dead if we went over the edge. Death was at my door again. Thanks to the Lord, we survived.

On May 31st, 1985, I retired from the Post Office. I got a security job at a cement plant that was on strike. Some of the security guys were getting lip from the strikers. One big security guard was pushing his weight around and he got waylaid at night by a two-by-four. Most of the guards were young and horsing around in the guardhouse. Talking to one of the workers, he asked me if I was a "Johnny-come-lately" security guard. I told him that I had just retried from the government as twenty-year security officer. "I understand about strikes," I told him. "I worked years ago and been on strike, also. This is just a job to make extra money like the men who want to get more money here. Just don't do anything in front of me, and there won't be any problem."

The guards were afraid to walk into the plant if there were three or four strikers standing in front of the door. I would walk right through them and enter the plant.

One day, I went to work and the guard said that they had found a case of dynamite and it was sweating. I asked, "Where is it?"

"It's still in the shed. But I have a stick here in the drawer."

"What are you, nuts! Get it the hell out of here!"

He gave it to the dynamite man.

The next day and employee had a stick painted red and gave it to the same guard. The guard spoke to one of the plant bosses and the guard got fired for being stupid. There were things being stolen and it was being done by a couple of security guards, so we lost the contract.

I have a twelve-by-fifteen roof patio, no sides, and I will build the bottom three sides. The south side window height will be 45 inches and the width 56 inches. The two east side windows will be 32 by 68 inches. The north side window will be 46 inches by nine feet long. The door on the south is a standard door width.

I backed into our new pear tree that I planted. I got some nails and put it back together and said nothing to my wife. A week went by and my wife said that the pear tree was not doing so good. A couple of more days passed by and she said we'd have to take that tree back. She went to dig it out and asked me how those nails got in the tree; they were not there before. I said 'it beat's me' and started to laugh.

About three hundred and twenty feet on the south side we had Arizona Cypress that went dead, and I cut them all out, some I had to pull out with a backhoe. I then planted trees and other kinds of plants.

We owned five acres with a cabin that we shared with our daughter. One weekend we watched a fire that came within a half-mile from the cabin. Two years later, the fire department stopped the fire fifteen feet from the cabin. A couple of years later we sold it at a loss.

We joined the Lions club in Lucerne Valley and I started out as range master of the target range. I was the first range master to charge for use of the targets. I pushed to have spots of cement put in where trap shooters could stand. I worked myself up to second vice president. I was also a member of Lucerne Water Board. I am a lifetime member of DAV --- Disabled American Veterans --- and Veteran of Foreign Wars, American Legion, the Moose Club, past member of Sons of Italy, and past member of the Eagles. I was also active in the Sea Scouts and Boy Scouts in my younger days, and in Little League Baseball.

I recall another time when we went to Big Bear with my wife and daughter looking for wood. My wife and daughter stayed by the truck. I walked into the woods deeper and deeper, and down a couple of gullies. I got confused and started back. I got back to the road but not at the same place. I could see my wife and daughter about a quarter-mile up the road. They said they were calling and I didn't answer and it was snowing, so my daughter broke the window and began blowing the horn and I still didn't hear them. So my daughter put a pile of rocks where the pick-up was as a marker. They were going to leave and get help just as I appeared. I never said a word about the broken window. I said that I wasn't lost because I came back to the road. What would have happened if the truck was gone and I walked up the road the wrong way? Would I have become lost? I was lost; I just got lucky.

With the increase in water rates, I started cutting back on our lawn. First, I had to cap off about sixty water heads and put down black plastic and get tons and tons of peat stones to cover the plastic. I still have a small lawn by the patio. The two timers still take care of all of the trees except for the far rear end of the lot on the south corner. This area has water heads. All we have to do is turn the valve on by hand. I had very little grass to cut so I sold my lawn tractor.

My health was doing fairly good until 1990. About 3 a.m. I got up to go to the bathroom and hemorrhaged. I thought it was my piles and went back to bed. In the morning, I hemorrhaged again and knew it wasn't my piles. There was a lot of blood. I went to our doctor and he sent me straight to the hospital. A doctor came and gave me blood and lasered the ulcer. I had been having trouble with my stomach ever since World War II. The first two years after I left the service, I was on goat's milk; and, I hate goat's milk. The surgery helped quite a bit.

In 1991 I saw a doctor for my prostate. He said it had to be reamed out, so I said, "Okay, which hospital?"

He said, "Right here in my clinic."

After surgery I had trouble passing my water. He inserted a tube into my penis and no water. He did that three times. I was now in a lot of pain and still no water. He got a metal rod that was about eighteen inches long and entered my penis again. I passed water and blood all over me. And that's the way he sent me home. My penis was sore for two weeks.

I went back after two days and asked, "Did you take a biopsy?"

He said, "No."

"Why not? Now you don't know if I have cancer or not."

"We are going to take a PSA test."

I had the test and went back to his office and asked for the results.

"You have a high reading. Somewhere in your prostate you have cancer."

I spoke to my wife. "Let's go back east and visit Mother and family and your family because this might be my last visit. When we come back I will see Doctor Jake."

Our visit was fine; we said nothing about the cancer to my mother. When we came back to California, I went to see Doctor Jake and had another PSA test that came back normal. When Doctor Jake examined me he said, "Your prostate was not cut out, all he did was to clear a little area so you could pass your water. If he had taken it out, your sperm would not come out of your penis. You don't have cancer. Your high reading was too soon after your surgery."

This shoemaker was sued two years later by another patient and lost but he is still a doctor. It is now fourteen years later and I am still free of cancer. Thank God.

One day our daughter told us to get our passports because she and her brother were paying for a cruise for our 50th wedding anniversary. Our daughter, Patricia, drove us to San Pedro where we boarded a Jubilee Cruise ship with Carnival Cruise lines. Our daughter paid for the cruise. She told the booking person not to place her parents with old people.

We toured Puerto Vallarta and Ensenada but a hurricane kept us from visiting Matzatlan and Cabo San Lucas. The hurricane was trailing us, which was circling around eighty miles per hour and sixty miles behind us. We were taken twenty miles off course into the ocean to avoid the worst of it. We did feel the strong winds. And there was more excitement: the ship hit a six-ton whale and we felt the jar. I told my wife that someone fell out of bed to calm her down.

I met another woodcrafter on the ship and we've been in touch ever since. There was another couple who went out of their way that they almost didn't make it back onboard the ship again. They were searching to buy us a 50th year Anniversary card. She had to have one made. We are still in touch with them, eight years later. This gift from our children we will never forget.

My wife, daughter, her girlfriend Rose, and I had an airplane ride to Cancun, Mexico. One of our tours brought us to the pyramids; it had 365 steps. My daughter, Rose and I started to climb the steps but my wife stayed at the bottom. Rose asked Patricia where I was. Patricia knew I was way up ahead of them. The steps were narrow and very slippery and I had leather soled shoes. Coming down you would go sideways to avoid slipping. When I got down I didn't see my daughter and I was just going back up to get her but she had come around from the other side. She told us that there was a big chain on that one side to help people get down without slipping. We learned more there than you could learn in school --- a good trip.

Having a close call of death in February 2003, my wife wanted to go back east to visit both sides of the family. While there my sister reminded me what Mother told us many years earlier. Mother was on her way home with my brother and I in a buggy, when two men tried to rob her. They tried a simple robbery because they thought Mother was carrying the money that Dad got for his fireworks display. Mother had a secret hiding place in the buggy and pulled out a .38 pistol and the men ran off. Mother went to my godfather and told him that two men tried to rob her and she knew who they were. Godfather and a couple men picked them up and delivered them to the police. They were glad the police had them and not my godfather.

When we still lived on Swan Street, we ran a grocery store with living quarters in the rear. Dad had come home late and Mother had his supper ready for him and said she was going to turn the lights off. With the house dark, she heard a noise in front of the store. She got Dad and told him there was someone in front of the store. Dad got the heavy frying pan and went behind one counter while Mother went behind the other counter creeping real low. She saw one guy start to make a circle in the glass window. That's when she fired the .38 pistol and heard him yell and swear. He was caught a block away and taken to the hospital. This all happened when the punk, Baby Face Nelson, was around. Mother thought it was him.

While visiting back in Buffalo, we decided to go to the town of Lawtons with my two brothers and wife. This was the town where the Indian wanted to kill me. The house was still there. It was remodeled: no front porch or store windows, no lean-to in the back. The store had burned down and no sidewalk. The railroad depot was gone and the saloon was still there but not as a saloon; it was now a gift shop. The bar had all the gifts on it and was run by an Indian. We talked about the old days and I spoke to the owner of the house and told him I had once lived there. The old red factory was there. It was now being used to pasteurize the milk from all the farmers from Lawtons and the nearby towns. Every morning the kids of this town would go there and drink all the free milk that they could drink, and the mothers of Lawtons got free milk to take home.

I wanted to visit the farmer that was good to us and who raised the prize-winning Black Angus cattle. I was surprised to find it run-down with no one on this former ranch. I wished I had time to find out what happened to this great family.

October 4th, the day before our 56th year of marriage, we were at our daughter's home because she was going to take us to the airport so we could catch the flight to Gulf Port,

Mississippi. My combat outfit was having their 58th anniversary. My wife didn't feel well and I rushed her to the nearby hospital. We were there all night. In the morning, we had to catch the seven o'clock flight so we left the hospital at five a.m. It was a tight squeeze and we met the flight. Our poor daughter didn't get much sleep. My wife's problem was the blood pressure patch.

While in the Houston, Texas, airport, we were sitting waiting for our flight to continue to Mississippi for my reunion, an airplane captain from Continental saw me and came to shake my hand. He had seen the words Bronze Star on my hat. He congratulated me for a job well done. Hundreds of people were watching.

We celebrated our 56th wedding anniversary and my 58th year reunion. This was my first reunion. I didn't know the 85th Division was having reunions. There were about ten men that showed up from Co. F 339th Infantry. Some of the old soldiers could not make it. I met one soldier who was a BAR man. He and I captured the German officer. Our next reunion was planned for 2004 in Washington DC.

At a casino in Gulf Port, Mississippi, while we were having lunch, this young man and his wife came to our table. He excused himself for disturbing our lunch but he wanted to shake my hand also for doing my part. He was in civilian clothes but he told me he was a helicopter pilot. Later he hit a jackpot for $2000 dollars.

On October 5, 1946 was the best thing I ever did and that was to marry my wife, Ida. Through thick and thin, she was always by my side, never complaining about hardships of me being sick many times and unable to work for nine and a half years. She helped me through the fractured pelvis, the spinal fusion --- she was always there. The girl I met when she was eight and I was ten; we were meant to be.

October 31, 2004, I had a bad dream. Walking down a road I came face to face with a big African male lion. We both stopped and he gave a big grow, and I came forward. I pulled my handgun and fired two shots into him as he leapt. I fell backward and put two more shots under his head. My heart was beating so hard and fast that it woke me up. I got out of bed and checked my pulse and it read ninety. I went to the kitchen and got some water and did some coughing. The pressure in my chest went down some. I ate some crackers and went back to bed. At 1:15 a.m., I didn't want to wake up my wife. In the morning, I called the Blue Cross registered nurse and asked for some information. I was told to go to the emergency hospital, which I did.

After a few tests, I was told I needed a stress test and to go to my heart doctor for the testing. They said I would be in for hours if I did the stress test in the hospital. I saw Dr. Elder and passed the test and was given 0.4 mg of nitro to put under my tongue if it happened again. Dr. Elder said a bad dream can hurt a healthy heart. God was with me one more time.

We enjoyed a family reunion July 30th, 2004, at our home in Lucerne Valley with three brothers, two sisters, a sister-in-law, my older brother Frank, who I hadn't seen in fifteen years, and his wife, Myra; my sisters Frances and Julia, brothers Lewis and Bob, and our daughter Patricia. Our son, Anthony, was unable to make it. My wife, Ida, did all the cooking, a fantastic cook. Frank and Myra had come from Georgia; the rest came from New York and Santee, California.

On August 10th my wife and I drove to Santee where our daughter had three tickets to fly us to San Francisco for my 80th birthday and Ida's 78th --- our daughter's gift to us. The plane was over an hour late and the shuttle had a near collision. We went to see the Liberty ship and went onboard. I showed my wife and daughter, if this had been my ship, where I was lying down on April 11th, 1944, when the German aircraft attacked us. A picture showed the area. Yet here we were, sixty years later, just like my reunion with my combat outfit in Washington, DC visiting the World War II monument. These memories I would cherish forever.

But I was to have one more close call in December 5th, 2004, while finishing my book. I had another bout with pneumonia and went into emergency at St. Mary Medical Center in Apple Valley. My health has been a bit shaky at times, like any surviving war veteran, but I plan to be here for many more years to come.

2

3

4

5

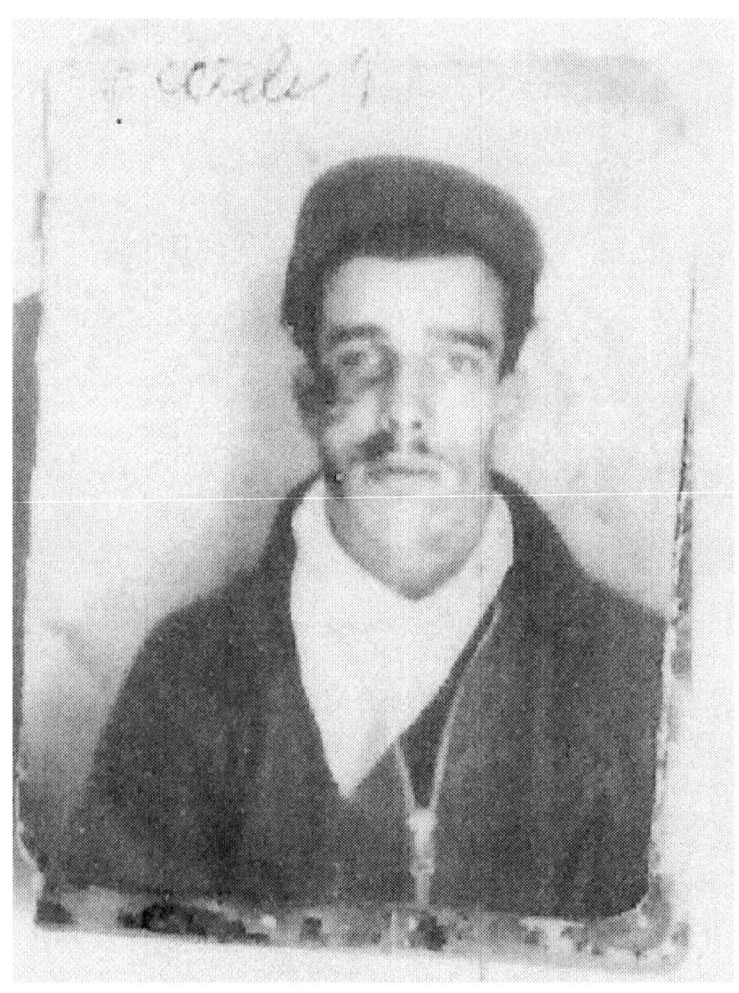

6

7

8

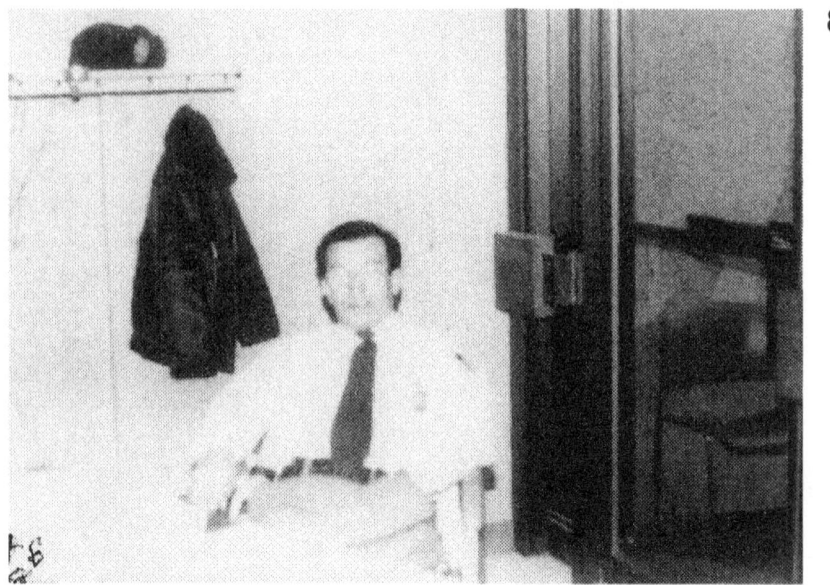

9

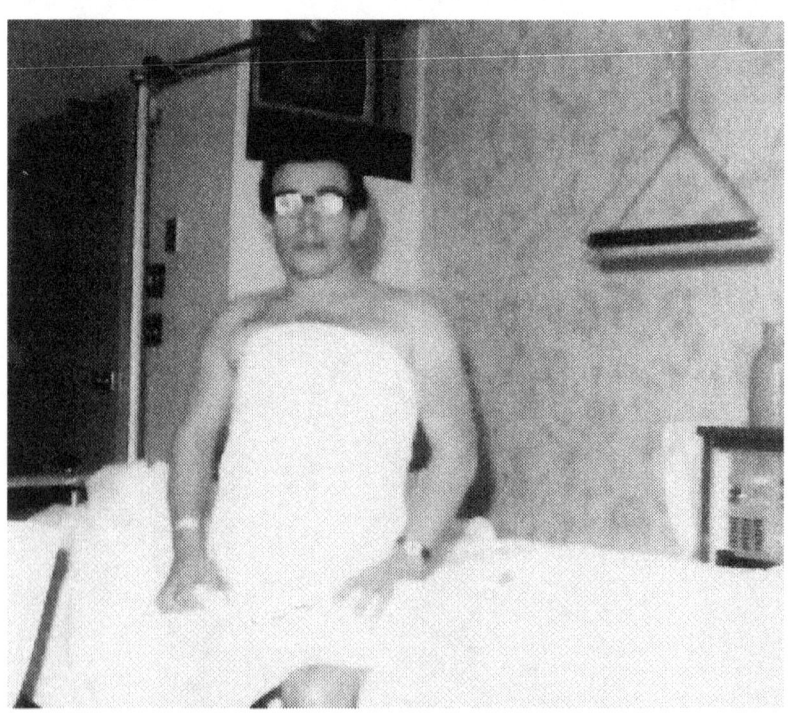

10

11

12

13

14

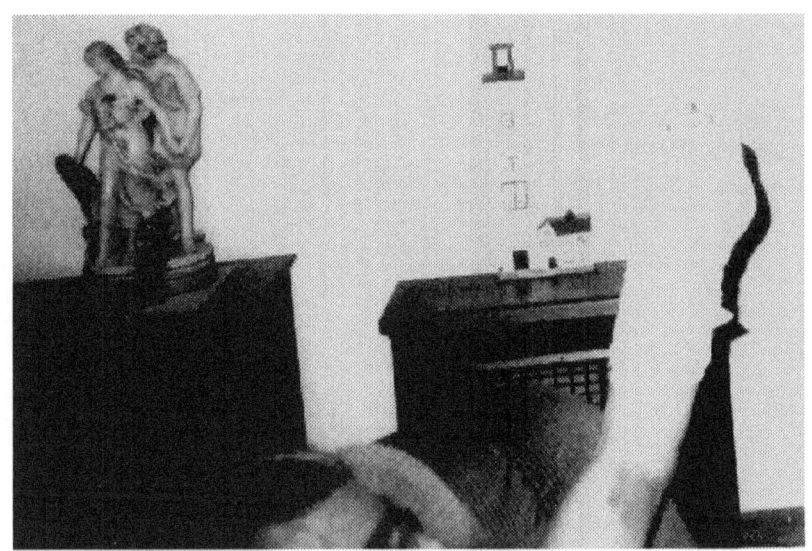

15

16

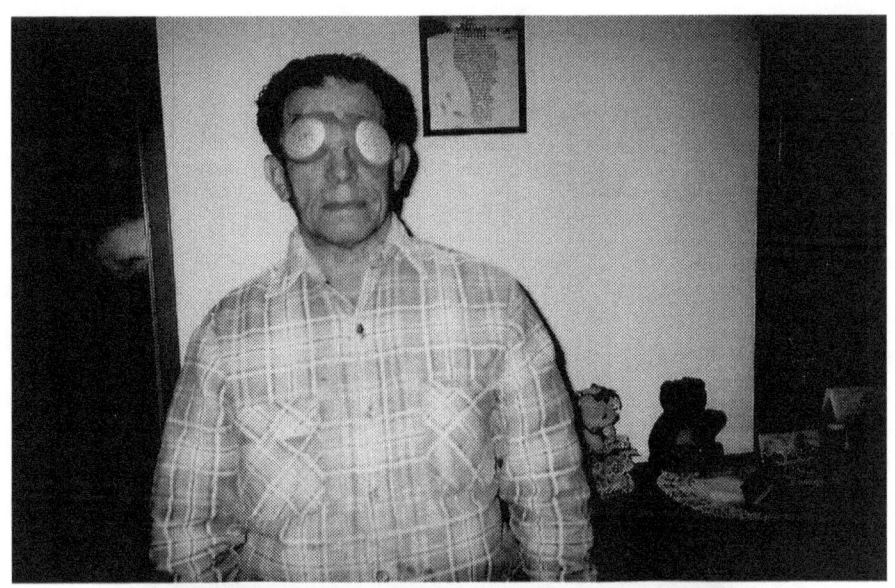

Thinking of Survival

Each day in combat there is a very good chance that it could be your last day, and each day you survive, it's a blessing. I had a close brush with death in my eighty years, non-combat and combat, and here is my list:

1. Last rites given twice before I was two years old
2. Pulled from the path of a streetcar before five years old
3. Fire in a well tile ****
4. Attacked by Indian with a knife when I was about eight years old
5. Knocked out when diving into a creek at sixteen years old
6. Working on railroad and was missed by train in dead of winter
7. Working at Bell Aircraft: fell through a security roof with four soldiers pointing guns at me
8. Soldier dropped an eight pound rifle on my head
9. Attacked by German aircraft (combat)
10. While checking a dead soldier, a sniper tried to get me (combat)
11. Dug in a minefield (combat)
12. Zeroed in on by a sniper when checking on forward area (combat)

13. Fighting a house fire; my wife wrapped my head in a wet towel to keep my hair from burning

14. Robber hit me on the head with a pipe

15. Lightning came through one window and out the other, close enough to singe my blanket as I was laying down

16. Pinned between two trucks; laid-up for nine and a half years

17. Oil stove smoking; dog woke us up at 3 a.m.

18. I fell and my head hit a metal plate, knocking me out

19. Car rolled over twice

20. While out on lake, storm came up, and boat's motor quit

21. Car swerved around two cars waiting for a signal light change and hit me on driver's side in the intersection

22. Car rammed me from behind while waiting for a signal light

23. Spinal fusion: needed eight pints of blood

24. Second fusion after first fusion broke: three pints of blood

25. Penicillin reaction: fell to the floor

26. Bowling ball hit me on the head and I passed out

27. Bicycle accident: lost two and a half hours of my memory

28. Tree fell and hit me on the head

29. Potentially non-fatal accident: dirt in combat caused scars in my eyes

30. Potentially non-fatal accident: working on grinder, metal dust in my eyes, more scars

31. Potentially non-fatal accident: bowling ball fell on my big toe on my right foot

32. Potentially non-fatal accident: boat anchor fell on same toe

33. Potentially non-fatal accident: stabbed myself in left wrist while working

34. Potentially non-fatal accident: cut little finger with band saw; finger saved

35. Contracted Hepatitis C from first spinal fusion; this is still hanging over me

36. Brush with death: doctor gave wrong medicine; I passed out twice

37. Contracted pneumonia for the ninth time in Feb. 2003

38. Lost brakes coming down mountain road from Big Bear Lake

39. Laser surgery for ulcer and hemorrhaging

End Note

In my 80 years of life I have a memory that can't be erased. I believe in perseverance, family, and trusted friends, above all. Believe in yourself. If you find yourself in a situation like I lived through, my life story might help you. Never give up. There are good days and bad days; one never knows what tomorrow will bring. Just like the sky, each day is different.

It's not that you have to survive with each close death, but that you have to live and let each near death be a memory. That's why I wrote about all the things I did in life.

Life is a challenge.

Along the fantastic journey of my life I met many people who are life-long friends. I have a loving wife and family, a granddaughter and two great grandchildren. I wouldn't trade my life with anyone. It's been a great adventure. I will live each day to the fullest, like I always have in the past, with an open mind and thankful for my 80 years, and hopeful for many, many more years of life.

*****   *****   *****

No matter what happens in one's life, you must try to be calm. That's easy to say. Being calm, you can think better; it just may help you survive.

--- Anthony Pasqualetti